"Miller's strong love for reading and her desire to develop lifelong readers is inspiring. She is crafty in her way of sweeping her students into her reading world. This is a great read that should encourage teachers to take a closer look at the readers in their classrooms and the way in which they teach reading and support them."

—*Arlyne Skolnik, Reading Teacher, West School, Long Beach NY*

"The Book Whisperer (I love the name!) was both inspirational and incredibly practical. I highlighted many passages to share with my students and teachers and I plan to use this as a text next year when I teach my undergraduate reading methods course."

—*Patricia M. Cunningham, Professor of Education, Wake Forest University*

"Miller's new book, *The Book Whisperer*, is a breath of fresh air in this era of teacher-dominated reading test preparation lessons. She sets forth both an argument and evidence for immersing kids in reading as the alternative to the often mindless reading lessons offered in hopes of improving test scores. She writes about her own 6th grade classroom where students are expected to read at least 40 books each year and her stories will convince you that it is time to focus on teaching children rather than teaching books or stories. She will convince you that it is time to stop assigning book reports, whole class novels, vocabulary lists, quizzes, and worksheets and, instead, give students the opportunity to choose what they will read (within limits). She will also persuade you to allocate the school time actually needed to read 40 books in a given year. This is a powerful and practical book, one that will support you as you change your classroom for the better while helping you understand how to overcome current classroom cultures where some children learn and many learn to hate reading."

—*Richard L Allington, Ph.D., University of Tennessee*

"Donalyn Miller's practical ideas about children and books are sound. In an age of test-driven curriculum, reading this book will remind teachers, administrators and parents why giving reading back to the students is the right thing to do."

—*Dr. Carol D. Wickstrom, Associate Professor of Reading, University of North Texas*

"In *The Book Whisperer*, Donalyn Miller deftly describes the inherent need children have to engage with books, intellectually and emotionally. The book is a timely and rare gift for teachers in this era of teaching for high-stakes assessments—Miller actually chronicles the path to reading for 'intrinsic motivation' we seek for all children, but seldom observe."

—*Ellin Oliver Keene, Author/Consultant*

"Miller is one of those teachers you always wanted for your children. She understands how to teach reading, but knows that is not the same thing as knowing how to LOVE reading. She explores the sources of that love—a feeling for a certain place, a certain time of day, a certain friend, a certain dream. Reading is being surprised, intrigued, captured, removed from reality to other places you want to revisit, often. Few authors have ever conveyed this as well to parents and teachers as Miller does here."

—*Jay Mathews, Washington Post education columnist and author*

"This book reminds anyone—who is lucky enough to have loved a book—what classrooms and kids have lost in our frenzy to 'cover' content and standardize student performance in the name of reading. This is a primer of the heart on how to make reading magical again."

—*Carol Ann Tomlinson, William Clay Parrish, Jr. Professor of Education, University of Virginia*

Jossey-Bass Teacher

Jossey-Bass Teacher provides educators with practical knowledge and tools to create a positive and lifelong impact on student learning. We offer classroom-tested and research-based teaching resources for a variety of grade levels and subject areas. Whether you are an aspiring, new, or veteran teacher, we want to help you make every teaching day your best.

From ready-to-use classroom activities to the latest teaching framework, our value-packed books provide insightful, practical, and comprehensive materials on the topics that matter most to K-12 teachers. We hope to become your trusted source for the best ideas from the most experienced and respected experts in the field.

Published by Jossey-Bass
A Wiley Imprint
One Montgomery Street, Suite 1200, San Francisco, CA 94104-4594—www.josseybass.com

Jossey-Bass books and products are available through most bookstores. To contact Jossey-Bass directly call our Customer Care Department within the U.S. at 800-956-7739, outside the U.S. at 317-572-3986, or fax 317-572-4002.

Jossey-Bass also publishes its books in a variety of electronic formats. Some content that appears in print may not be available in electronic books.

Library of Congress Cataloging-in-Publication Data

Miller, Donalyn.
  The book whisperer : awakening the inner reader in every child / Donalyn Miller ; Foreword by Jeff Anderson. –1st ed.
        p. cm.
  Includes bibliographical references and index.
  ISBN 978-0-470-37227-2 (pbk.)
  1. Reading (Elementary) 2. Reading (Middle school) 3. Children–Books and reading.
  4. Motivation in education. I. Title.
  LB1573.M4938 2009
  372.6–dc22

                                                                2008055666

Printed in the United States of America

FIRST EDITION

PB Printing   20 19 18 17 16 15

Donalyn Miller

The Book Whisperer

Awakening the
Inner Reader in
Every Child

Foreword by Jeff Anderson

JOSSEY-BASS
A Wiley Imprint
www.josseybass.com

To Don,
my whisperer

Contents

Foreword

DONALYN MILLER'S voice is one of a real teacher. She whispers practical ideas, validation, and fundamental truths about teaching independent reading that are often lost in the din of ever-increasing test prep mantras. Out of fear of failure or pressures from outside our classrooms, we let go of the very strategies and routines that could make our students succeed at reading, thinking, and writing. Donalyn's critical eye sees what is happening to our classrooms. She laments how reading classes often become places without room for reading—authentic reading, as educators call it. As Donalyn notes, The National Reading Panel rejected the value of independent reading, but we simply can't. Why would we focus on inauthentic reading? Seriously.

The Book Whisperer is practical and passionate. Donalyn Miller has no complicated scripts, endless prescriptions, or pie-in-the-sky quick fixes. In clear and accessible ways, she shares the nuts and bolts of an independent reading program, offering suggestions for how to begin and maintain a workshop approach that won't make you pull your hair out. Have you ever wondered how to inspire a reluctant reader? Donalyn has simple practical advice. Have you ever wondered how to get your students to keep a record of their reading? Have you figured out how to encourage students to respond to reading without squeezing every drop of joy out of it? Donalyn has. One page at a time, she reveals how any teacher can artfully listen and respond to their students and take them to new heights of reading achievement and pride that may seem out of reach. She reinforces with class-created charts, note taking, student talk, and writing activities how easily our instruction can flow from our students' interactions with text, with us, and each other.

Donalyn is a friend with whom you want to kick off your shoes and talk for a while. She is also the kind of friend who never beats around the bush. She says exactly what she thinks and what she knows. She doesn't hold back. Her credibility is borne of experience and experimentation, failure and refinement, gut instinct and heart-felt concern, stubbornness and an ability to let go. She teaches us through her classroom stories and her students' voices. She gives us information to stretch, shift our focus, and make our class a path to life-long, joyous reading.

Reminding us that reading instruction is about one thing—reading—she stays constant and true to the practices she has honed in her classroom. There are no worksheets, computer tests, incentive programs, packaged scripts or scripts parading as professional books here. Donalyn Miller speaks for the joy of reading, reminding us what we should fight for—students with their hands and eyes and minds on real, free-choice books—and what we should let go.

Donalyn's personal story will cause you to reflect and refine your reading program. Whether she is talking about types of readers and solutions for teaching them, reminding (or introducing) you to the simple brilliance and applicability of Camborne's conditions of learning, or explaining why we should fight for independent reading time in our classroom, the voice of a real teacher comes though.

Curl up with this good book. Personally recommended titles are the best, aren't they? Just like Donalyn and her students recommend books to each other, I am recommending this book to you. Read it right now. You will be inspired to open a book and to amp up or restart your independent reading program both for you and your class. I was.

Within these pages, Donalyn nudges us to reflect on how our students are engaging in our reading program, against the backdrop of her own story. She gives us a vision of what an effective reading program looks like. And how easily it can be done. Of course, anything this wonderful takes some effort, but any meaningful effort never feels like a struggle. With this book, we simply relax into the flow of words and discover all the places we can go.

Jeff Anderson

Introduction

I AM NOT A READING RESEARCHER. I am not a reading policy expert. I do not have a Ph.D. What I am is a reading teacher, just like many of you. My source of credibility is that I am a teacher who inspires my students to read a lot and love reading long after they leave my class. I require my students to read forty books during their time in my sixth-grade classroom, and year after year, my students reach or surpass this reading goal. Not only do my students read an astounding number of books, they earn high scores on our state's reading assessment, the Texas Assessment of Knowledge and Skills (TAKS). I have not had one student fail the state assessment in four years, and an average of 85 percent of my students score in the 90th percentile, Texas's commended range. I have taught students of all economic and academic backgrounds, from the children of non—English speaking immigrants who struggle with the English language to the children of college professors. The conditions I create in my classroom work for all of them.

When teachermagazine.org asked me to respond to readers' questions for their "Ask the Mentor" column in the fall of 2007, motivating students to read mountains of books was my source of credibility to them and to the thousands of readers who made that column so popular. Teachers, administrators, and parents flooded teachermagazine.org Web site with questions about picking books, getting students interested in reading, and developing conditions in classrooms and living rooms that would encourage children to read.

Due to the obvious demand for practical information about creating readers, the editors at teachermagazine.org next offered me a long-term stint writing a blog titled "The Book Whisperer." The blog is a place where I can fly my free-choice reading flag and discuss the issues that reading teachers contend with daily: national, state, and district policies that mandate what we teach, the limited instructional time we are given to teach, and the eternal quest to inspire our students to read.

Why is the need to motivate and inspire young readers such a hot-button issue? Why do teachers and parents cry out for information on how to get children to read? This topic is in the limelight because so many children don't read. They don't read well enough; they don't read often enough; and if you talk to children, they will tell you that they don't see reading as meaningful in their life.

The field of reading research produces study after study attempting to explain why emergent readers are not learning to read well by third grade, why intermediate students are not interested in reading, why secondary students read less and less with each passing year they are in school, and why so many students cannot comprehend the information in their textbooks or pass standardized tests. Instead of re-examining the foundation of sand on which so many federal and state reading programs were built, the 2000 Report of the National Reading Panel, "Teaching Children to Read," policymakers ask for more money and beg us all to give these programs more time (National Institute of Child Health and Human Development, 2000). The children cannot wait. They do not have more time. While Washington policymakers, state and district boards of education, and administrators scramble to figure out what is best practice for getting children to read, crafting program after program in which they claim to have the answers, these children are graduating and breathing a sigh of relief that they never have to read a book again.

We have worked so hard to develop systems to teach reading, yet I claim that we had no justification for systematizing an act like reading in the first place. The only groups served by current trends to produce endless programs for teaching reading are the publishing and testing companies who make billions of dollars from their programs and tests. It is horrifying that the people who have the corner on getting children to read—children's book authors, parents, and teachers—get the least credit monetarily or otherwise.

I believe that this corporate machinery of scripted programs, comprehension worksheets (reproducibles, handouts, printables, whatever you want to call them), computer-based incentive packages, and test-practice curricula facilitate a solid bottom line for the companies that sell them. These programs may deceive schools into believing that they are using every available resource to teach reading, but ultimately, they are doomed to fail because they overlook what is most important. When you take a forklift and shovel off the programs, underneath it all is a child reading a book.

In 2000, the National Reading Panel left independent reading off their recommendations for improving reading instruction, stating, "The Panel was unable to find a positive relationship between programs and instruction that encourage large amounts of independent reading and improvements in reading achievement" (National Institute of Child Health and Human Development, 2000, pp. 12–13). It puzzles me that an initiative with the purpose of improving students' reading achievement leaves out independent, free-choice reading. Stephen Krashen, respected researcher, activist, and author of *The Power of Reading*, identifies fifty-one studies that prove that students in free-reading programs perform better than or equal to students in any other type of reading program. Krashen found that students' motivation and interest in reading is higher when they get the opportunity to read in school. Krashen's findings deliver the message that every other activity used in classrooms to teach reading had better get the same results as independent reading—not only in terms of reading achievement but also in terms of *motivation*—or it is detrimental to students.

I was asked at a recent speaking engagement how I can justify to my principal the hours of class time I set aside for students to read. Pointing to my students' test results garnered gasps from around the room, but focusing on test scores or the numbers of books my students read does not tell the whole story. It does not tell half of the story. You see, my students are not just strong, capable readers; they love books and reading.

Building lifelong readers has to start here. Anyone who calls herself or himself a reader can tell you that it starts with encountering great books, heartfelt recommendations, and a community of readers who share this passion. A trail of worksheets from a teacher to their students does not build a connection with readers; only books do.

The fact that educators coined the terms *real reading*, *authentic reading*, and *independent reading* to differentiate what readers do in school from what readers do in life is part of the problem. Why does it have to be different? Why is the goal of reading instruction disconnected from reading in the rest of a student's life? When did reading become such a technocratic process that we lost the books and the children in the debate? I am convinced that if we show students how to embrace reading as a lifelong pursuit and not just a collection of skills for school performance, we will be doing what I believe we have been charged to do: create readers.

No matter the stage of your teaching career, *The Book Whisperer* has something to offer you. Each chapter explores one aspect of my instruction, which fits into a cohesive plan for creating a classroom culture in which students will read. Topics include:

- *My personal reflections about being a lifelong reader.* The most powerful component of my teaching practice is my joy in reading and my reading experiences. Follow my journey as a reader, and reflect on what reading means to you.

- *Practical strategies you can implement in your classroom.* Investigate the nuts and bolts of setting up a classroom library, designing reading requirements, carving out reading time, and altering your instruction to align with the habits of real readers.

- *Anecdotes and quotes from students who are becoming readers.* The best lessons I have learned about teaching reading have come from my students. Let their words about living a reading life and how schools often prevent them from becoming readers guide and inspire you. All the student quotes in this book are from my sixth graders.

- *Whispers.* These brief interludes, dispersed throughout the book, present activities that I have used early, midway, and late in the school year to promote dialogue about reading between my students and me.

So why write another book on getting students to read? Am I a hypocrite for denouncing the reading industry and then participating in it by producing another book claiming to have answers? Although I have read about and implemented many of these ideas myself, including how to create reading and writing workshops and teach comprehension strategies, *The Book Whisperer* has something different to offer. Toni Morrison has said, "If there's a book you really want to read but it hasn't been written yet, then you must write it." (Jacobs and Hjalmarsson, 2002, p. 37). That is what this book is—the book that I always wished I could find when I was learning how to teach. I needed a book that showed me how to connect my love of reading to my teaching of reading and how to use what I already knew about being a lifelong reader to encourage my students to read, but I could never find one.

I imagine there are some readers of this book who will get validation for the great practices they already use to motivate their students to read. Bask in the validation. You deserve it. There are some who want the practical tips I provide. Do what great teachers have always done: steal whatever ideas you can use. There are a few of us, though, who need a change of heart, a paradigm shift about what reading should be—both for our students and for ourselves. I hope you can find it. Maybe this book will inspire you to start looking. No matter what kind of reader you are, know that I value you and welcome you here.

CHAPTER 1

There and Back Again

What we have loved

Others will love

And we will teach them how

—William Wordsworth

Reading has helped me a lot with writing my book. All of the books I read gave me ideas and thoughts for writing. Without books, I would not be writing a storybook today.

—Jonathan

ONE OF MY FIRST MEMORIES is of learning to read. My mother owned an electrical contracting business, and, as a single mother, sometimes had to take me on road trips with her. As we drove the highways between Texas and Arkansas, she read road signs to me, praising me whenever I "read" a McDonald's or Texaco sign. Barely three years old, I was undoubtedly parroting back the colors and sign shapes I recognized, but it was not long before I was reading on my own. My mother was my world, and she brought reading into it. Thinking about how I walked through my childhood with my nose perennially stuck in a book, I sometimes wonder whether she regretted turning me on to reading so early.

My mother worried that because I was holed up in my room reading, I would become socially stunted. To the contrary, reading would connect me to the most important people in my life. My husband, Don, is a reader. I knew we were destined to be together forever when, on our third date, I discovered he had read—and loved—one of my then-favorites, Stephen King's post-plague battle between good and evil, *The Stand*. He often paces in front of the bookcase in our living room, calling out to me, "What have you got for me to read?" Books are love letters (or apologies) passed between us, adding a layer of conversation beyond our spoken words. Neither one of us could imagine spending our life with someone who did not read.

Some of my favorite memories with our two daughters revolve around time spent sharing books, too. Don, Celeste, and I read the entire Harry Potter series out loud together as each book was published. We started the first book when Celeste was nine, and she turned seventeen shortly after we finished the last. I cried and cried not only because Rowling's epic was over but because I saw that the journey of raising our beautiful child was also nearing its end. When our power went out for three days during recent spring storms, our nine-year-old, Sarah, begged us to read ghost stories to her by candlelight, claiming that these were, in her words, "the best stories" to read in a house filled with eerie silence and creepy shadows.

Even my friendships hold book love at their core. Mary, my best friend, and I bonded as moms and readers while escorting our children to the public library every Wednesday for two summers. We were the only library patrons who needed a Radio Flyer wagon to carry out all of the books we checked out each week. Mary and I talk about a great many things—our children, our parents, our spouses, politics, what we heard on NPR—but we always make time to talk about our cherished books, too.

I am a reader, a flashlight-under-the-covers, carries-a-book-everywhere-I-go, don't-look-at-my-Amazon-bill reader. I choose purses based on whether I can cram a paperback into them, and my books are the first items I pack into a suitcase. I am the person whom family and friends call when they need a book recommendation or cannot remember who wrote *Heidi*. (It was Johanna Spyri.)

My identity as a person is so entwined with my love of reading and books that I cannot separate the two. I am as much a composite of all of the book characters I have loved as of the people I have met. I will never climb Mt. Everest, but I have seen its terrifying, majestic summit through the eyes of Jon Krakauer and Peak Marcello. Going to New York City for the first time, at forty, was like visiting an old friend I knew from E. L. Konigsburg's *From the Mixed-Up Files of Mrs. Basil E. Frankweiler* and Mark Helprin's *Winter's Tale*. I wanted to go to the Metropolitan Museum of Art, hide in the bathroom until it closed, and look for angels. I know from personal experience that readers lead richer lives, *more* lives, than those who don't read.

My obsession with books and reading defines my life, and when I chose teaching as my second career (following my first one as a bookkeeper), I walked into my classroom convinced I would share this passion with my students. No matter what else I had to offer them, I could offer my enthusiasm for books.

It wasn't that easy.

Wake-Up Call

The summer before my first teaching assignment, I spent a month planning a unit for one of my favorite books, *The View from Saturday*, by E. L. Konigsburg. This story of an emotionally and physically damaged, but inspiring teacher, Mrs. Olinksi, and her extraordinary students, who grow to love and respect each other over the course of a school year, was powerful to me and, I thought, would resonate with my sixth-grade students. I wanted to be caring but strong, like Mrs. Olinksi, and encourage my students to develop bonds with one another the way her students, the brilliant Souls, did in the book.

I read the book again and, in the margins of my copy, made careful notes of conversational points to discuss. I created extension activities that tied in with the events in the book's plot: we would investigate the migration habits of sea turtles, host tea parties, write calligraphy, and discuss the main characters' cultural differences. I crafted leveled comprehension questions for each of the book's chapters, diligently varying the difficulty of the questions according to the domains of Bloom's Taxonomy, just as I had learned to do in my college methods courses. I selected key vocabulary words that

I felt students should know. We would make our own crossword puzzles! The unit was a work of art, a culmination of everything I had learned about good teaching, and I was proud of it.

It was a disaster.

Lost in the Wilderness

As often happens to well-intentioned teachers, my plans fell apart when my students showed up. The fact that I ever taught this way haunts me still. The students did not connect with the characters to the extent that I had imagined they would. They slogged through the book, asking, "How long should my responses be?" and "Would you look at my drawing for question 9 and tell me if this is what you want?" The children were compliant and did the work, but their hearts were not in it. I could tell they were not emotionally or intellectually getting much from the book. They were robots, trudging through the unit and completing the assigned activities. Reading was work, another job to finish in the daily grind of school. I could not wrap my head around what was wrong. The book was great. The unit was thoughtfully planned to interest students, but the children were not engaged.

I noticed that the few students who were avid readers already would rush through the unit activities only to ask, "I am done with my work; may I read my book now?" Horrified, I recognized that my classroom had become the same kind of classroom I reviled in my memories of school—a reading class with no place for readers. I remember hurrying through the required books in school (and all of the accompanying work) so that I could get back to my books, too.

Distraught, I took my observations to the more experienced teachers at my campus, asking for help. To my chagrin, this is what I heard: "The children are just lazy. They will do the minimum to get by." Or "Most of them hate to read. I have to drag my students through every unit."

They also told me that *The View from Saturday*, a story about sixth graders, was too difficult for my sixth-grade class. According to my colleagues, my students hated to read and those who loved to read would do so in spite of my teaching, not because of it. I recognized that this Newbery Medal—winning book was not the problem; how I taught it was. So what was I going to do about it? There had to be a better way.

Where Am I Going?

It has been said that teachers teach how they were taught. When I was in school, the students all read the same book and did the same activities. This is how I taught reading, too; all of the teachers at my school did. No matter what we heard in college about authentic reading, there was little support for teaching reading any way other than the whole-class novel, everyone on the same page at the same time. When you walk into a teacher supply store or browse a resources catalogue, the glut of canned materials for novel units reinforces that this is the best means to teach reading.

If my students deserved more, they did not expect it. For them, reading in school had always looked the same: read the chapters and complete endless activities on each one; take a test on the book when you finally finish it; and start the process over with another book. Reading more than a few books a year was not possible for these students because these cookie-cutter units took so long to get through. Unlike the promising name of the Epiphany Middle School in *The View from Saturday*, that year held few divine revelations for me. I spent the rest of it trying to design what I thought would be more engaging novel units. I piled on more fun activities and art projects, never acknowledging that my students were doing less reading and writing. My instruction was still about my goals and my assigned texts. I hoped that if I worked harder, did a better job of designing what I taught, I would finally get it right. But secretly, I despaired that I would never inspire my students to find the rapturous joy in reading that I did.

On the Path

Looking back on those days now, I see that the answer was right in front of me. On those rare opportunities when I allowed my students to choose their own books, their interest in completing assignments was sparked; I just failed to make the connection. Letting students choose their own books for every assignment was not done in any classroom I had ever been in, and I did not know how to design instruction that would accomplish the goals of my curriculum and still allow students to make choices. I blamed my failure to inspire my students to read on my inexperience as a teacher. It never occurred to me that I was trying to build a reading program from broken materials. My methods were flawed, not my implementation of them.

As my first school year progressed, I found myself spending more of my planning periods in the doorway of our assistant principal (and future principal), Ron Myers. He was a great listener who recognized my hunger to succeed with my students and my desire to forge connections between them and books. He urged me to talk with Susie Kelley, a teacher of twenty years and the curriculum facilitator at our school, whose classroom became a refuge for me. Even with her extensive knowledge of reading and writing practices, Susie was always searching for methods to improve the literacy instruction in her classroom and still struggling to get it "right." Susie lives by the credo "If you ever think you have all the answers, it's time to retire." She encouraged me to keep trying and to keep learning.

And of course, I continued to read. With so many questions rattling around in my head about how to teach reading, pursuing answers by soaking up every book I could find on the subject was a logical step for me. Lost, wandering in a teaching wilderness, I allowed the acknowledged leaders in the field of literacy to guide me. How I was teaching reading, it dawned on me, was likely the problem. Susie pointed me toward books on workshop teaching; I found other books in bookstores and professional catalogues. I hungrily devoured the words of great teachers who had tapped into successful methods of teaching reading. It was there that I began to discover what wasn't working about my practice and how I might go about fixing it.

I tabbed and underlined every profound idea and practical tip I could glean from these experts; Post-it notes, like quills, stuck out of countless pages in my methods books. Four porcupine books I read that year, in particular, shaped my teaching philosophy and put me on the path I still travel today: Nancie Atwell's landmark book on workshop teaching, *In the Middle*; Irene Fountas and Gay Su Pinnell's practical guide to scheduling, designing lessons, and assessing within a workshop classroom, *Guiding Readers and Writers (Grades 3–6): Teaching Comprehension, Genre, and Content Literacy*; Ellin Keene and Susan Zimmerman's *Mosaic of Thought*, which distills reading comprehension down to its key components; and Janet Allen's folksy, realistic guide to working with adolescent readers, *Yellow Brick Roads: Shared and Guided Paths to Independent Reading 4–12*. Through these wise practitioners, I began to see how I could bridge the gap between my visions of the perfect reading classroom and how I thought I could get there.

I transformed my classroom into a workshop, a place where apprentices hone a craft under the tutelage of a master. I learned that being the best reader and writer in the room is not about power and control. Instead, I must be a source of knowledge that my students access while learning how to read and write. Instead of standing on stage each day, dispensing knowledge to my young charges, I should guide them as they approach their own understandings. Meaning from a text should not flow from my perceptions or, God forbid, the teaching guide; it should flow from my students' own understandings, under my guidance.

KEY COMPONENTS OF A READING WORKSHOP

- *Time:* Students need substantial time to read and look through books.
- *Choice:* Students need the opportunity to choose reading material for themselves.
- *Response:* Students should respond in natural ways to the books they are reading through conferences, written entries, classroom discussions, and projects.
- *Community:* Students are part of a classroom reading community in which all members can make meaningful contributions to the learning of the group.
- *Structure:* The workshop rests on a structure of routines and procedures that supports students and teachers.

Source: Atwell, 1998.

Reading is both a cognitive and an emotional journey. I discovered that it was my job as a teacher to equip the travelers, teach them how to read a map, and show them what to do when they get lost, but ultimately, the journey is theirs alone.

My goal was for students to read and write well independently. If I never demanded that my students show me what they learned through their authentic words and work, what assurances would I have that they had internalized what I taught them? As long as my teaching was about my activities and my goals, students would be dependent on me to make decisions and define their learning for them. The practices of literacy leaders I discovered during this period validated my instincts that students should spend the majority of their time in my class reading and writing independently, and their publications gave me the research substantiation I needed to defend these beliefs. I realized that every lesson, conference, response, and assignment I taught must lead students away from me and toward their autonomy as literate people.

The lack of control over reading choice was the problem with my novel unit on

The View from Saturday and the others I taught that year. Giving students choice over their reading was foreign to every classroom I had ever sat or taught in. I began to see how independent reading and student choices could coincide with my curriculum. I never taught a whole-class novel unit again. Armed with my newfound knowledge, I dove into my second year of teaching with a structure on which I could teach reading that made sense to me, both as a teacher and a reader. It was better that year, so much better. I had a plan.

Granted, it was someone else's plan.

Going Forward, Sort of

With a workshop structure in place, my students were more engaged in reading and writing and more enthusiastic. Instead of teaching books, I taught comprehension strategies and literary elements that students could apply to a wide range of texts. I implemented the reader's notebook, taken straight from Fountas and Pinnell's model, in order to manage my students' independent reading; set up reading requirements for my students based on genre as a path to choice; and assigned book talks to replace the dreaded book report. I photocopied mountains of reading strategy worksheets, lists of reading response prompts, and workshop management forms. I bought every picture book that my workshop mentors recommended.

The structure of the workshop drove everything that I did, and it left me frustrated. Instead of finding my own way, I was now bent on channeling those master teachers. If I was unable to follow the step-by-step lesson plans laid out by reading experts because of the unique needs and personalities of my students, my own teaching style, the time constraints of my instructional block, or access to resources, I felt like a failure. I kept striving to make my class look like the ones I read about, full of engaged children and exemplary teachers, and when I fell short, I did not know what to do except to try harder. Making the workshop work became more important than the readiness or interest of my students or me. You see, while I searched for the key to being a master reading teacher, I forgot what workshop teaching was all about—my role as master reader—which goes beyond just following a lockstep sequence of lessons that some distant guru had advised me to use.

The funny thing is that I knew how to inspire readers thirty years ago because I knew what made reading inspirational for me. These days, I share with my students what no literacy expert could ever teach me. Reading changes your life. Reading unlocks worlds unknown or forgotten, taking travelers around the world and through time. Reading helps you escape the confines of school and pursue your own education. Through characters—the saints and sinners, real or imagined—reading shows you how to be a better human being. Now, I accept that I may never arrive at teaching paradise, but as long as I hold on to my love of books and show my students what it really means to live as a reader, I'll be a lot closer than I once was. Finally, this was my epiphany.

CHAPTER 2

Everybody Is a Reader

To acquire the habit of reading is to construct for yourself a refuge from almost all the miseries of life.

—W. Somerset Maugham

I have learned that you can't hate a book till you've tried it! Bring it on.:-)

—Emily

YES, I GREW A LOT those first two years, but I still had a lot to learn about being a responsive teacher. What I thought my students needed each week when I wrote my lesson plans was not as important as how I responded to their needs when they expressed them to me.

On the first day of my third year of teaching, after I delivered a lengthy lecture on class rules, homework demands, and locker and restroom procedures to my new class of students, I stopped to ask whether they had any questions. One boy raised his hand and, glancing at the wall of books that forms the class library on one side of the room, asked, "When will we be allowed to check out books?" I was taken aback. I never saw myself as a teacher who did or did not allow students to read. Was there a magical, undetermined time when it was acceptable for the children to begin reading? Well, no, there wasn't. Surprising my students and myself, I blinked a few times and blurted, "Now. We will check out books now."

Tentatively, students got out of their seats. After listening to my rules lecture for the past fifteen minutes, I think they were amazed that I would let them touch my books without some additional diatribe. I can imagine their thoughts. "What, no talk of jelly stains and dog-eared pages?" "No threats of tongue-lashing if we misplace a book?" "She spent three minutes telling us how to go to the bathroom, but she is just going to turn us loose on those books?" A few pioneers thumbed through the bins. When I saw one girl select Sharon Creech's journey of self-discovery, *Walk Two Moons*, I asked her whether she had read it before. She had, so I directed her to one of Creech's more recent books, *The Wanderer*. A group formed around me.

Students clamored for recommendations, asking me whether I had read the treasured books many were now clutching in their hands. I raised a copy of one my favorites—*The Thief Lord*, Cornelia Funke's magical tale of Viennese street orphans—over my head, and asked, "Has anyone read this? I loved it." Two boys, digging through the fantasy section of the library, raised their hand. I declared, "Two, only two? That's not enough!" I went into my cabinets, where I kept crates of my book sets, many of them from my whole-class unit days. Dragging out a tub and snapping off the lid, I doled out copies of *The Thief Lord*. When that tub was almost empty, I popped open others, which held *Stargirl*, by Jerry Spinelli; Gordon Korman's *The Sixth Grade Nickname Game*; and, yes, *The View from Saturday*.

Students grabbed books and gave book recommendations to each other and to me. I was talking to one child about books and then another and another. I located some index cards and had students jot down their names and the titles of the books they were checking out. My classroom looked like the floor of a bizarre stock exchange, with students excitedly waving cards and calling out book titles. Jace, a student from that class, still remembers the experience: "I walked out of there with three books that day, and they are still on my list of favorites," he told me recently. At the time, Jace was not an enthusiastic reader, but he got caught up in the wave of excitement from his classmates and me.

Since that landmark day, when I decided to listen to what my students needed and not tell them what I thought they needed to hear, I have always started the school year with this book frenzy. By making book selections and sharing past favorites the first activity in which we engage as a class, I emphasize the prominence that reading will hold all year. I also reveal to students that I am knowledgeable about books and that I value their prior reading experiences and preferences. The book frenzy sets the tone for my class. Everyone reads every day, all year long.

In those first days, I never preach to my students about their need to read. I never talk to them about the fact that many of them do not like to read, struggle with reading skills, or have not found reading personally meaningful. If I were to acknowledge that these excuses have merit, I would allow them to become reasons for my students not to read. They pick books on the first day, and they read. If the book they chose during that first frenzy does not work for them, they abandon it and choose another. Choosing not to read is never discussed. It is simply not an option. Although I never state it outright to my students, my mandate that they read and the enthusiasm I show for books sends a powerful message. I want my students to know that I see each of them as a reader. All students in the class are readers—yes, with varying levels of readiness and interest—but readers nonetheless. I must believe that my students are readers—or will be readers—so that they can believe it. The idea that they can't read or don't like to read is not on the table.

Embracing their inner reader starts with students selecting their own books to read. This freedom is not a future, perhaps-by-spring goal for them, but our first accomplishment as a class. Why does choice matter? Providing students with the opportunity to choose their own books to read empowers and encourages them. It strengthens their self-confidence, rewards their interests, and promotes a positive attitude toward reading by valuing the reader and giving him or her a level of control. Readers without power to make their own choices are unmotivated.

Types of Readers

Students come into our classrooms with all sorts of reading experiences, many of them not positive. By middle school, students have an image of themselves as readers or nonreaders. Students who do not read see reading as a talent that they do not have rather than as an attainable skill. We label students according to their success on standardized reading tests and their personal motivation to read. Students who have not met minimum standards for test performance are called "struggling readers." We classify students who don't read books outside of school or require substantial goading to pick up a book as "reluctant readers." Lord, help the student with both labels.

I need to put forward more encouraging terms for my students than the negative popular terminology *struggling* and *reluctant*. Where is the hope in these terms? I prefer to use positive language to identify the readers in my classes. Peeking into my classroom, I see sixty different readers with individual reading preferences and abilities, but I consistently recognize three trends: developing readers, dormant readers, and underground readers.

Developing Readers

The type of students whom I call *developing readers* are commonly referred to as *struggling readers*. For any number of reasons, including inadequate reading experiences or learning disabilities, these students are not reading at grade level. They have difficulty understanding the reading material in every aspect of their lives. By the intermediate grades, the majority of developing readers have been in reading intervention programs and tutoring for several years. Their standardized test scores are low, and some have failed at least one state assessment. These students do not see themselves as capable of becoming strong readers, and they (and their parents) are beginning to despair, perhaps thinking that reading competence will remain forever out of their reach.

Why do developing readers continue to struggle in spite of every intervention effort? Well, the key might be in the amount of reading these students actually do. Reading policy expert Richard Allington explains in *What Really Matters for Struggling Readers* that when he examined the reading requirements of Title I and special edu-cation programs, he discovered that students in remedial settings read roughly 75 percent less than their peers in regular reading classes. No matter how much instruction students receive in how to decode vocabulary, improve comprehension, or increase fluency, if they seldom apply what they have learned in the context of real reading experiences, they will fail to improve as much as they could.

The fact that students in remedial programs don't read much has serious consequences for developing readers. Students who do not read regularly become weaker readers with each subsequent year. Meanwhile, their peers who read more become stronger readers—creating an ever-widening achievement gap. Dubbed *the Matthew effect* by Keith Stanovich, referring to the passage in the Bible (Matthew 13:12) that is often interpreted as "The rich get richer and the poor get poorer," this gap indicates that no matter the intervention, developing readers must spend substantial instructional time actually reading if they are to attain reading competence.

Here is why I have hope for children who have fallen behind and why I call them developing readers instead of struggling ones: these students have the ability to become strong readers. They may lag behind their peers on the reading-development continuum, but they are still on the same path. What they need is support for where they are in their development and the chance to feel success as readers instead of experiencing reading failure. They also need to read and read. Time and time again, I have seen a heavy dose of independent reading, paired with explicit instruction in reading strategies, transform nonreaders into readers.

Kelsey

The first time I saw Kelsey's name, it was on "the list"—the list of students who had failed the state assessment three times but were being promoted to sixth grade anyway, on the assumption that with the right mix of tutoring intervention and strong reading support, they would be able to catch up. Kelsey was not just a struggling reader; she was a defeated one. Kelsey feared that she was going to fail the state assessment again and be retained in sixth grade. Her mother was supportive but did not really know what to do, either. She read to Kelsey and read with her. She spent hours at the dining room table working with Kelsey on practice items for standardized tests from the workbooks that Kelsey's teachers sent home, and she remained vocal and involved in Kelsey's school life, but none of her efforts had helped improve Kelsey's reading ability to the degree that she had hoped.

Although Kelsey could trill off a staggering list of strategies for attacking reading on a standardized test, she did not have much experience reading books on her own because she spent most of her time during reading instruction practicing test-taking and comprehension strategies and thus had few opportunities to apply and practice what she had learned with real books. It was clear that the rescue recipe of equal parts tutoring, test practice, and parental support that is commonly served to developing readers was not working. Kelsey was way behind the other students in her class and, without making up the reading miles she had missed, had little hope of catching up with them. When Kelsey found out that I expected her to read a lot in my class, she confessed to me that she did not know how to choose a book that was appropriate or interesting to her, and that she struggled to read the books that her classmates read because those books were too hard for her.

Learning that Kelsey loved animals, especially horses, I steered her toward books in the Animal Ark and Heartland series, which are written at a third- or fourth-grade level, because I knew she would be able to read these easily and have a positive experience with the books. As Kelsey developed experience as a reader, her confidence grew and she read book after book. As Kelsey continued reading, the difficulty and sophistication of the books she chose increased naturally and she became a stronger reader. She made amazing progress and was reading close to grade level by the end of the year. Most important, Kelsey discovered a love for books and saw herself as a good reader for the first time. Kelsey received reading intervention services from our reading specialist all year, just like always; went to tutoring after school, just like always; worked with her mother at home, just like always; but this year, she also read every single day.

In the spring, spotting Kelsey and her mother in the hall after school, I ran over to tell them the great news: "Kelsey passed the Reading TAKS with flying colors!" Kelsey's mom welled up with tears, and Kelsey clutched me, sobbing with relief, "Thank you! Thank you!" I felt a bit emotional myself. How sad that Kelsey needed the validation of that test score to prove she was a good reader. After all, she had read forty-two books that year. Connecting Kelsey to books and adding a cup of heavy reading were the missing ingredients in the rescue recipe. Kelsey has not been in a reading intervention program since, and in eighth grade, she earned a commended scholar rating on the state test. She has never stopped reading.

Dormant Readers

Because of the demands of standardized testing in the world of No Child Left Behind and the drive to make sure all students reach a minimum level of reading achievement, developing readers take up a disproportionate amount of the resources in a school. While teachers focus their instructional efforts on the students who are at risk of failing state assessments or classes, there is a whole group of readers who are taken for granted. I feel that the vast numbers of readers who move through our classrooms unmotivated and uninterested in reading are as troubling as the developing ones. But in many cases, whether these students read is not a concern as long as they pass the state test every year.

These reluctant or—to identify them more positively—dormant readers are the students who read in order to pass their classes or do well on state tests but who never embrace reading as a worthwhile pursuit outside of school. These students read their assigned books, do their assigned activities, and drop the books when weekends or summers arrive and they don't have to read anymore. Reading is work, not pleasure. Without support for their reading interests and role models who inspire them to read, these students never discover that reading is enjoyable.

The burden of poor reading skills or a disability that impedes their ability to read well is not what prevents dormant readers from being enthusiastic readers. After all, the majority of people who graduate from school are not lagging behind in their reading to the extent that they cannot get along in the world. So why do so many people who can read choose not to do so? I think that dormant readers might become engaged readers if someone showed them that reading *was* engaging.

I believe that all dormant readers have a reader inside themselves, somewhere. They simply need the right conditions in order to let that reader loose—the same conditions that developing readers need: hours and hours of time spent reading, the freedom to make their own reading choices, and a classroom environment that values independent reading. Children love stories, which offer the escape of falling into unknown worlds and vicariously experiencing the lives of the characters. Children's attachment to the story arcs in video games and television programs bears this out.

What students lack are experiences that show them that books have the same magic. They have never been given the chance to discover the worlds that books can contain. Because so many students' reading choices are dictated by their teachers, they never learn how to choose books for themselves. How can they shape a self-identity as a reader if they never get the chance to find out what they like? If you are a student and your entire class is reading one book together (a common practice), what do you do if you don't like that book? How would that uninteresting book color your view of books in general? By denying students the opportunity to choose their own books to read, teachers are giving students a fish year after year but never teaching them to go near the water, much less fish for themselves.

Because dormant readers are good enough readers, able to jump through the reading hoops in the typical classroom, they don't garner much concern from teachers—but they should. Students who don't read, even if they are capable of completing reading tasks at school, run the risk of falling behind students who read more than they do. After all, Mark Twain reminds us, "The man who does not read great books is no better than the man who can't." At the beginning of the year, I find that dormant readers constitute the largest segment of readers in my classes.

Hope

Hope provides an example of what a dormant reader looks like on arrival in one of our classrooms. Despite the fact that Hope succeeded in her schoolwork and excelled on state assessments every year, she did not see herself as a reader and found few books worth reading. I placed book after book in her hands, hoping she would find one that she liked. Hope took my offerings dutifully at first. Some she read, and some she snuck back onto the shelf. Slowly, she began to find books that spoke to her eclectic spirit. She gravitated toward books with bizarre settings and fantastical elements, like *The Giver*, by Lois Lowry, and *Coraline*, by Neil Gaiman. When Hope began to express preferences for certain types of books, I had seeds of information that helped me lead her to more books. I have a penchant for fantasy, science fiction, and traditional literature (legends, myths, and fairy tales). Hope and I connected over our shared love of Greek mythology in particular, so I suggested books to her that I knew she would enjoy reading. The more books

I recommended that she liked, the more Hope trusted me to suggest books.

What Hope needed was a chance to browse through lots of books every day and an opportunity to read widely. I remember how reluctant Hope once was when I see her these days, legs slung over a chair in our school lobby, waiting on her ride home, nose buried in a book. She is still a regular visitor to my library, even though she left my class long ago.

Underground Readers

Underground readers are gifted readers, but they see the reading they are asked to do in school as completely disconnected from the reading they prefer to do on their own. Underground readers just want to read and for the teacher to get out of the way and let them. I was this type of reader in high school. While my teacher spent six weeks dragging the class through Nathaniel Hawthorne's *The Scarlet Letter*, a book I finished in a week, I whiled away the time by creeping myself out with Stephen King's *Salem's Lot* and mind-traveling to Polynesia through James Michener's *Hawaii*. In accordance with the unwritten contract between my teacher and me, she overlooked my obvious boredom with her class and I kept my mouth shut and my head down, reading from my own book, which I kept hidden inside my desk. I took sly pride in the fact that I earned an A+ on the final for *Huckleberry Finn* when I had not even finished the last third of the book. The teacher belabored the plot and her interpretation of it for so long that I knew what she would ask us on the test without even reading the book.

While teachers scurry to support students who are still developing their reading skills and wonder what they can do to motivate the dormant readers who do not like to read, underground readers are a subset whose needs go unaddressed. These children are the ones who come into our classes as avid readers. The opportunity to graze through stacks of books, picking those that look interesting to them and getting the time to read for hours in school is the dream of every underground reader, but underground readers have had to accept that this freedom is not going to happen in most of the classrooms they sit in year after year. These students have such advanced reading abilities and sophisticated tastes that few teachers design instruction around their needs, preferring instead to develop a curriculum that supports most of the other students, who are reading at or below grade level.

Randy

Some underground readers are the bright and shining stars of the reading classroom, the ones who other students know are readers, who reinforce for teachers that some of their instruction must be working because these students do so well on the teacher's assessments. Of course, these students would have done well on these assessments from day one. Or underground readers might be students like Randy, who, by most measures of school success, failed my class. (I was still stifled by other people's expectations for my teaching back then.) Randy was always lugging around some massive tome with a dragon on the cover. I knew he was a reader, but Randy could not have cared less about completing any assignments; he just wanted to read. Because his grades were so low, my school's guidelines required that I put Randy in my after-school tutoring group, even though we both knew he did not need it. While his mother, my teaching partners, and I held innumerable conferences that year, discussing what we were going to do with Randy, he sat in the hall, reading happily.

Predictably, because he read constantly, Randy scored in the 95th percentile on the state reading test and was promoted to seventh grade. I am confident that he is still out there somewhere, reading a four-hundred-page book and checked out mentally from his reading class. I let Randy down. Is there one of us who is not haunted by the memory of a child we failed? I wish I could be his teacher again so I could show him that I get it now. I would let him read those dragon books all year and never try to force him to conform to my transitory reading goals for him. I would look for ways to use the books he does read to meet my instructional goals, like I do now.

Randy read every day, committed to his own vision of what reading meant to him and unwilling to compromise with external forces like teachers that infringed on his core reading values. This should have been enough for me. Randy is what a real reader looks like, and my efforts to force him to conform to my short-term goals for his reading when he was already on the path to a lifelong identity as a reader were futile. Underground readers who do or don't comply with the teacher's concept of what reading is should not have to wait for lunchtime, summer break, or graduation for their reading life to begin.

I only have to look at my classroom now to see how far this change of attitude has taken me. Once I accepted that my primary aim was to instill the life habits of readers in all of my students, habits that students like Randy already had, my teaching finally aligned with my life view of what reading should look like for readers. This vision extends beyond students sitting in reading class and encompasses the reading identities students already possess when walking into my classroom. One such underground reader, Alex, educated himself for years by being a covert classroom reader. Free to read whatever he wanted, Alex declared our class "reading heaven." He persisted reading books propped inside his desk all year, even though he didn't have to. I teased him, declaring that since I had invented this trick thirty years ago, he owed me royalties every time he did it.

Testing the Teacher

The fact is that scores of the children who enter our classrooms are students who like to read or once did, before years of traditional reading instruction focused on comprehension worksheets, book reports, and whole-class novel units made the experience of reading boring and painful. Michelle's reading reflection entry reveals her beliefs about reading prior to my class:

> When you told us that you expected us to read 40 books this year, my first thought was: She. Is. Crazy. I used to hate to read more than Aunt Eleanor's potato salad (and believe me, that stuff is pretty nasty). I think part of it was the fact that the only books I read last year were books that the school required us to read. We would do worksheet upon worksheet of reviews and vocabulary on every single chapter.

That I expect my students to read forty books a year is not the chief concern for many students. They usually want to know what activities I will ask them to do with the books they are reading, because worksheets, vocabulary tests, and book reports have always been the goal for every book they have ever read in school; never has it been for their pleasure or engagement. They have a tough time believing that I have not tied their books to a lot of teacher strings, so they quiz me, looking for the catch:

"How will you be grading this, Mrs. Miller?"

"Don't worry about grades. If you keep reading, you'll be fine."

"May I read books from home or only yours?"

"First, these are *our* books, yours and mine. Second, yes, you may read books from home."

"How will you know that we are really reading?"

"Trust me, I will know."

They don't have much confidence in me. If I am not going to quiz them on every book and monitor their every reading move, how will I control reading for them? School, for them, is about performing to the teacher's expectations and doing the work that the teacher requires.

Our students have no background in how a class can be different. They begin each school year filled with hope that this year will be more interesting and engaging than the last, and yet, the drudgery that surrounds reading continues, year in, year out. It takes time for students to get to know me and trust me and then to believe that they have as much reading freedom as I claim they do. When faced with the wall of books in my classroom, Corbin didn't feel anticipation; he felt dread:

> I remember the moment perfectly, Meet the Teacher night, I walk into my LA & SS [Language Arts and Social Studies] room and all I see are books. Then Mrs. Miller walks up and says we have a 40 book requirement. The first thing that pops into my mind is—book reports.

Conditions for Learning

What I did not know when I started teaching was that no matter how dynamic and well planned my instruction was, if my classroom was not a motivational environment for readers, my instruction was doomed to fail. Based on decades of classroom observations on the conditions that foster learning, Australian researcher Brian Cambourne identifies the following factors that contribute to successful learning:

- *Immersion:* Students need to be surrounded with books of all kinds and given the opportunity to read them every day. Conversations about reading—what is being read and what students are getting from their books—need to be an ongoing event. In my classroom, students have access to hundreds of books of all genres and reading levels and encouragement to read widely.

- *Demonstrations:* Students require abundant demonstrations on the structure and features of texts, how to use texts for different learning goals, and how to access the information in them. I teach daily reading lessons using authentic texts like books, articles, and textbooks, designing every lesson around the skills that readers really need to develop reading proficiency.

- *Expectations:* Students will rise to the level of a teacher's expectations. I expect my students to read every day and to read a large volume of books. Not only do I have high expectations for reading, I have high expectations for students' success. They are never given messages, either explicitly or implicitly, that I do not think they can accomplish any reading task.

- *Responsibility:* Students need to make at least some of their own choices when pursuing learning goals. Cambourne states, "Learners who lose the ability to make choices become disempowered." I set reading requirements for my students at a certain number of books per genre, but students have the freedom to choose which books they will read in order to fulfill the requirements.

- *Employment:* Students need time to practice what they are learning in the context of realistic situations. Every single lesson that I teach circles back to students' own reading, and students are given time daily to apply the skills they acquire to their own books, content-area reading, and research assignments.

- *Approximations:* Students need to receive encouragement for the skills and knowledge they do have and be allowed to make mistakes as they work toward mastery. I help students find books that are at their own reading level, even if it is below grade level, and publicly celebrate each reader's accomplishments as he or she moves toward more mature reading ability.

- *Response:* Students need nonthreatening, immediate feedback on their progress. By holding frequent conferences, requiring written response letters about their books, and discussing students' reading with them daily, I am continually providing encouragement, guidance, and validation for their reading development.

- *Engagement:* Even with all of the other conditions in place, engagement is the most important condition for learning and must exist in a successful classroom. Reading must be an endeavor that

  - *Has personal value to students:* Do students see a reason to read outside of the need to do so for school? Do students find any enjoyment in reading, or is it just a job?

  - *Students see themselves as capable of doing:* Do students see themselves as readers or nonreaders? Are they discouraged by reading failure in the past? Do they see themselves as able to learn to read well?

  - *Is free from anxiety:* Is reading weighted down with so many requirements for performance that reading is connected in students' minds with an obstacle course of work and, therefore, with stress? Have students been punished for not meeting mandates for reading at school?

  - *Is modeled by someone they like, respect, trust, and want to emulate:* Does the teacher model reading habits in his or her life? Do students respect the teacher as someone knowledgeable about reading? Has the teacher communicated to students that he or she sees students as capable enough to make some learning decisions?

I no longer spend the majority of my planning time crafting those glorious novel units. Instead, I focus my efforts on designing a classroom environment that engages my students, based on Cambourne's conditions for learning. We can spend hours determining what students should know and be able to do, crafting instruction to accomplish the desired results, but without considering students' right to an engaging, trustworthy, risk-free place in which to learn, what we teach will always fall short. Students must believe that they can read and that reading is worth learning how to do well. We have to build a community that embraces every student and provides acceptance and encouragement no matter where students are on the reading curve.

WHISPER
Student Surveys

SIGHING, I SHUT MY DOOR at the end of the day and enjoy the quiet of my second home, my classroom. It is the first week of school, and unaccustomed to talking and standing all day, my throat and feet are sore. I wander over to my desk, collapse a little too hard into my chair, and begin thumbing through the surveys my new students filled out in class.

Two piles await me. One is a stack of Reading Interest-A-Lyzer surveys. Created by Sally Reis, based on a form by Joseph S. Renzulli, the surveys ask students to describe their reading habits and their ideal language arts class. The other stack contains general interest surveys, modified versions of a survey created by Susan Weinbrenner (see Figure 2.1 and 2.2). Topics range from students' preferences in books, movies, and television programs to which famous people they would like to interview. Teachers frequently use interest surveys as a means to gain insight into the preferences and personalities of their students. In addition, I analyze these surveys for information that will help me encourage my students to read.

In order to make personal reading recommendations to my students, I need to learn about their past reading experiences and their interests both in and out of school. I mine these surveys for nuggets of information that will form the basis for book recommendations. Students may not be able to describe what types of books they might like to read, but if I have knowledge of their personal interests, I will be able find books that match a topic they enjoy.

<u>Interest Survey</u>

Thank you for answering this survey honestly, with thought,
and taking the time to explain "why" when it is asked.
This will greatly help us learn more about you and your
interests. We are looking forward to a great year!
— Mrs. Miller and Ms. Musgrave

Name: *Christina*

1. What kind of books do you like to read?

   I like to read Mystery books.

2. How do you get your news? What parts of the newspaper do you look at regularly?

   I watch the local news, and read the comics.

3. What are your favorite magazines or web sites?

   My favorite magazines are highlites, and adventure kids.

4. What type of TV programs do you prefer? Why?

   I like the soccer chanels because I can learn new soccer moves.

5. What is your favorite activity or subject at school? Your least favorite? Why?

   My favorite activity is P.E., and my least favorite subject is english.

FIGURE 2.1: *Example of a Student's Response to a Teacher's Survey*
Source: *Christina, grade 6.*

6. What is your first choice about what to do when you have free time at home?

   I practice soccer with my dad.

7. What kinds of things have you collected? What do you do with the things you collect?

   I used to collect rocks but not any more.

8. If you could talk to any person currently living, who would it be? Why? Think of 3 questions you would ask the person.

   I would talk to Mia Hamm because she's realy cool.
   1. Have you played soccer all your life?
   2. If so, have you always been good at it?
   3. Do you have any pets?

9. If you could talk to any person from history, who would it be? Why? Think of 3 questions you would ask the person.

   I would talk to Jesus because I've never met him and I wonder what he's like.
   1. What is your favorite food?
   2. What is your favorite animal?
   3. Did you ever have sleepovers when you were little.

10. What are your hobbies? How much time do you spend on your hobbies?

    My hobbie is soccer I usually spend 1hr every day acept on monday and friday.

FIGURE 2.1: *(Continued)*

<u>Interest Survey</u>

Thank you for answering this survey honestly, with thought,
and taking the time to explain "why" when it is asked.
This will greatly help us learn more about you and your
interests.   We are looking forward to a great year!
    — Mrs. Miller and Ms. Musgrave

Name: Rachel (Mrs. Miller's class)

1.   What kind of books do you like to read?

I like to read mysteries, historical fiction, and science fiction.

2.   How do you get your news? What parts of the newspaper do you look
     at regularly?

I like to read the sports section, and the front page of the newspaper.

3.   What are your favorite magazines or web sites?

I don't have favorite magazines or web sites I like to explore different things.

4.   What type of TV programs do you prefer? Why?

I like cartoons and kids shows. I like these programs because they are funny and usually interesting.

5.   What is your favorite activity or subject at school? Your least favorite?
     Why?

My favorite subject at school is a tie between science and math. My least favorite subject is Language Arts.

FIGURE 2.2: *Example of a Student's Response to a Teacher's Survey*
Source: Rachel, grade 6.

11. If you could have anything you want, regardless of money or natural ability, what would you choose? Why?

If I could have anything that I wanted I would have World Peace and the ability to fly. I would choose these because I've always wanted to be able to fly and World Peace would make it so much easier to study and learn about other cultures.

12. What career(s) do you think might be suitable for you when you are an adult?

I think that a career in comedy or acting would be suitable. I also think that a sports career or a business career would be reasonable.

13. If you could spend a week job-shadowing any adult in any career, which would you choose and why?

I would shadow my Uncle in a business career because I love to try to find ways to sell things!

14. Tell about your favorite games.

My favorite sports games include basketball and softball. Basketball is a very fun sport to play because you never know who will win! I like softball because it is fun to play with friends

15. What kinds of movies do you prefer to see? Why?

I like to see funny movies and action movies. I like to watch action because it keeps you interested during the movie. I also like to watch comedy because I can relate to some of it.

FIGURE 2.2: *(Continued)*

Shutting out the sounds of lockers slamming shut from the hallway, I focus on what whispers to me from their words. How can I reach each one through books? What books can I recommend that will inspire them to read more? What insight can I glean from the answers they have so dutifully recorded? Holding each child in my mind as I read, I try to match my initial observations of them with their written comments.

Christina

She is bouncy like Tigger, with an easy laugh and a cheerful personality. Even her ponytail bounces. Christina is smart, but she is already learning to mask her intelligence in the manner that so many adolescent girls do. I have noticed that she is not that enthusiastic about reading. Scanning her survey, I look for clues that will help me find enticing books for her.

What type of TV programs do you prefer? Why?

I like the soccer channels because I can learn new soccer moves.

What is your first choice about what to do when you have free time at home?

I practice soccer with my dad.

If you could talk to any person currently living, who would it be? Why?

I would talk to Mia Hamm because she is really cool.

Identifying Christina as a soccer fanatic is an understatement. She even lists Argentina as the country she would most like to visit because, she explained later, they have an "awesome" soccer team! I also notice that she lists English as her least favorite subject. Connecting her with books that tie in with her love for soccer is my obvious first step. Thinking for a moment, I remember that I purchased an *Eyewitness: Soccer* book over the summer because so many students in my class last year expressed an interest in the sport. Finding the book, I jot a note on a Post-it, asking Christina if she would like to be the first to read it. Since she is in my morning class, I walk over to her desk and put the book and note on top.

Rachel

Rachel is smart, like Christina, but she doesn't care if everyone knows it. Confident and easygoing, with a sharp wit, Rachel is a student others gravitate toward. I think she is good at being a social chameleon. She fits in well with other kids, but I wonder whether she shows much of who she really is. I wonder about this because it is hard to pin down her preferences from her survey answers (see Figure 2.2).

> If you could have anything you want, regardless of money or natural ability, what would you choose?
>
> *If I could have anything that I wanted I would have World Peace and the ability to fly. . . .*
>
> What career(s) do you think might be suitable for you when you are an adult?
>
> *I think that a career in comedy or acting would be suitable. . . .*

Although Rachel would pack books on a fifteen-year trip in space and spends time reading with her family, she lists language arts as her least favorite class. I wonder what the story is there. Perhaps she is an underground reader who has separated her reading life from her school life. I know from talking to her that she did not read much last year. If I could get her to read more, her influence with other students would help spread the reading vibe. I walk over to the class library across the room and start building a preview stack for Rachel, pulling books about kids like her, kids who have more to them than meets the eye: Paul from *Tangerine*, *Wringer's*

Palmer, *The Misfits'* Bobby and Addie, and my favorite loser-hero, Alfred Kropp. I build a tower of books and put them on her desk, too. She can preview the stack tomorrow and choose which books appeal to her.

• • •

I continue this process for an hour, channeling my gut and heart observations of the children, reading and rereading surveys, wandering back and forth in front of our book bins and grabbing book after book after book. For students in my morning class, I stack books right on their desk. For the afternoon group, I line the counter behind my desk with piles of books, Post-its marking the intended recipients. I will continue tomorrow and every day after until I have made preview stacks or pulled select titles for all sixty of my new students. Their needs as readers, as people, call to me from the pages of those surveys, and I whisper back with books.

CHAPTER 3

There's a Time and a Place

No matter how busy you may think you are, you must find time for reading, or surrender yourself to self-chosen ignorance.

—Atwood H. Townsend

*I read in class and that influences me reading
everywhere else.*

—Marilyn

SITTING CROSS-LEGGED on my bed, covers up to my chin, I
am reading Anna Quindlen's *Black and Blue*, the story of a woman
in an abusive marriage. The book is well written and riveting, and
I just can't put it down. An annoying knock at the door pulls me
out of my book, and I call out two words familiar to my loved
ones: "Last chapter!" Swap Quindlen's novel for E. L. Doctorow's
historical narrative *Ragtime*, and it could be me two decades ago.
No matter what else I may have to do—grade papers, fold laundry,
or catch up on e-mails—the siren call of my books is always there,
luring me back. Reflecting on her own lifelong obsession with
reading, Quindlen writes in *How Reading Changed My Life*, "Books are
the plane, and the train, and the road. They are the destination,
and the journey. They are home." I know that my life is marked
by the road signs of my beloved books, each one symbolizing who
I was when I read it, shaping who I have become. The uninitiated
might say that I am lost in my books, but I know I am more found
than lost.

This is what I want for my students, to lose and find themselves
in books. During their own busy days of soccer practices, Boy
Scouts and Girl Scouts, homework, and chores, they have little free
time to read, so I must make sure that I give them time to read
in class every day. After all, if I do not make time for them to
read in school, why should they make time for it in their life?

How much time are we talking about? My class starts every day
with independent reading time. At the beginning of the school
year, this time may be as little as fifteen minutes. I want students

to get used to the routine of starting our class this way. At the beginning of the year, before I start my conferences with them on a regular basis, I read, too. Students need a reading role model in front of them. I also want to make it clear to them that reading time is not an opportunity to talk to me about their homework or ask to go to the band hall. Nor is it free time to take care of personal errands or clean out a binder. Reading time is for reading. I value this experience so much that I set aside time for it every day, no matter what else we are doing. I joke to my students that if we had a twenty-minute class, it would be spent reading.

Time for Reading Is Time Well Spent

I express to my students that reading is not an add-on to the class. It is the cornerstone. The books we are reading and what we notice and wonder about our books feeds all of the instruction and learning in the class. At first, this reading time is my mandate for them. They read because I tell them to. I want to instill in them the daily habit. Like brushing their teeth, reading is a responsibility that my students understand I expect them to assume. Yet time spent reading feeds more reading. The more my students read, and grow into a community of readers, the more they want to read. As we move into the year full swing, I set aside a little more time each day for independent reading. By springtime, students spend about thirty minutes of our ninety-minute language arts block reading their independent books. My students do not even realize how much time they are reading each day. But I do know how much they value the time I give them to read because of all the groans and complaints I get when I announce that reading time is over. I often hear, "Mrs. Miller, can we have a day where we just read for the

> *Reading in class makes me read more at home and on the weekends because if I am caught in a book, I HAVE TO FINISH IT.* —**Molly**

whole class?'' In the spring, when half of my class was away at a band competition, we did just that!

No matter how long students spend engaged in direct reading instruction, without time to apply what they learn in the context of real reading events, students will never build capacity as readers. Without spending increasingly longer periods of time reading, they won't build endurance as readers, either. Students need time to read and time to be readers.

In *The Power of Reading*, his meta-analysis of research investigating independent reading over the past forty years, Stephen Krashen reveals that no single literacy activity has a more positive effect on students' comprehension, vocabulary knowledge, spelling, writing ability, and overall academic achievement than free voluntary reading. By loading the instructional day with traditional drill-and-kill activities such as weekly spelling and vocabulary lists and tests, grammar workbook exercises, and low-level comprehension assignments, all of which have a minimal or, in many cases, negative impact on student achievement, Krashen asserts that we are denying students access to the one activity that has been proven over and over again to increase their language acquisition and competence as communicators: again, free, voluntary reading. I have observed that my students are more likely to read a book at home that they have started reading at school. Free reading also liberates underground readers so they do not have to switch back and forth between their book for school and their own book.

The question can no longer be "How can we make time for independent reading?" The question must be "How can we not?" Since making independent reading the core of the reading program in my classroom, I have witnessed an increase in student achievement as well as a sharp increase in student motivation

> *I think it is great that we get to read in class each day. Sometimes, the best part of my day is getting to read for half an hour.* —**Bethany**

> *I try to take every chance I get to read in school because mostly school is quite boring. When I read in class it fills up the little hole in my heart (JUST KIDDING!!!).*   **—Jon**

and engagement. Students like Kelsey who have failed the state assessments pass them after a year of heavy reading. Students who previously had never read more than the few books they were required to read for class read book after book. What are the effects of intensive reading? Better writing, richer vocabularies, and increased background knowledge in social studies and science are natural outgrowths of all of the reading my students do.

Even if traditional instruction were able to provide equivalent gains, the improvement in students' attitude toward reading would be cause enough to devote substantial time to independent reading. My former students come back and tell me that time to read their own books in class is almost nonexistent in middle school and high school. Why aren't we giving students more time for independent reading in class? I hear many teachers say that they cannot set aside time for students to read because they have so much content to cover, but to what end? Because reading has more impact on students' achievement than any other activity in school, setting aside time for reading must be the first activity we teachers write on our lesson plans, not the last. It is said that we make time for what we value, and if we value reading, we must make time for it.

Stealing Reading Moments

> *Resolve to edge in a little reading every day, if it is but a single sentence. If you gain fifteen minutes a day, it will make itself felt at the end of the year.*
> —Horace Mann

Dedicating a large part of the instructional block for independent reading may seem impossible in our current standards-based world of high-stakes testing, but it is not. Even if you must follow a district- or school-mandated program that includes scripted drill activities and a lockstep curriculum, you can make time for independent reading. Thanks to a savvy principal, I have support for designing my entire class around independent reading, but I know that others may not have this freedom. There are creative ways, however, to carve out extra reading time for your students, even if you have a very structured routine, just by maximizing the moments of a typical class day.

Classroom Interruptions

I teach two double blocks of language arts and social studies per day, about two hours and thirty minutes of instructional time per class. Recently, I tracked the interruptions of my classroom instructional time over the course of a week. I logged fourteen visits from office personnel to deliver messages, forgotten lunches, and notes that needed to go home; nine phone calls from other staff members; two hallway discussions of student behavior; and one impromptu parent conference. All told, my students and I lost forty minutes of instructional time that week, and this is at a school that makes an effort to limit interruptions during the class day. This list is not atypical for most teachers—no doubt, you recognize each of these distractions. And each time these interruptions occur, we have to stop teaching and then regain our footing in order to pick up where we left off. The greater issue of limiting classroom interruptions is a systemic one, but how to recoup lost time with students is within a teacher's reach.

In the first few years of my teaching, nothing filled me with dread the way that a ringing classroom telephone or knock on the door did. Not only did I lose my train of thought, but it was hard to pick up the thread of my students' engagement when we had to stop and start again. I also struggled to keep one eye on my visitor and one eye on students who might take advantage of the situation and misbehave. Maintaining control of a classroom when

I am distracted by interruptions requires that my expectations for students' behavior be clear so that my students know what to do. During the early weeks of school, my students practice getting out their books when there are classroom interruptions. I start by prompting students to read when we are interrupted, but as the year progresses, students internalize this procedure, first as a habit, but eventually as a desire to steal more reading time. Their books call to them all of the time now, too, you see.

Bell Ringers and Warm-Ups

When evaluating an instructional practice, I first ask myself, "What purpose does this activity serve?" No matter how flashy, fun, or pervasive in classrooms an activity is, my overarching goal is to increase students' reading ability. Any pursuit that does not accomplish this specific goal goes out the window.

Like a lot of teachers, I used to prepare assignments such as editing exercises or writing prompts and have them on the overhead projector for my students to complete as they entered the classroom. On the surface, these activities were designed to engage students in some sort of literacy instruction or practice, but we all know what a bell ringer or warm-up is truly meant to do: get students in their seats, quiet and working, as soon as possible. Evaluating these activities with a critical eye, I realized that every nonreading activity was wasting precious minutes of reading time daily.

Take a look at a common classroom warm-up lesson: students are asked to look for grammatical and punctuation errors in a scripted sentence. Correcting the sentence may take five minutes. Discussing their corrections with students and providing feedback might take another ten minutes. Considering how little of this direct grammar instruction actually transfers to students' writing (Alsup & Bush, 2003; Thomas & Tchudi, 1999; and Weaver, 1996), these fifteen minutes would be better spent reading, an activity that has been shown to improve students' writing and grammar (Elley, 1991, cited in Krashen, 2004).

With instructional time at a premium in every classroom, we cannot afford to waste any of it. Research has confirmed that independent reading is the better use of our time. Students in my class enter my classroom each day, get out their books, and start reading. Not only are students quiet and working (the implicit goal of all warm-up activities), but they are engaged in a productive endeavor that improves their reading performance. The amount of time I save by not having to plan and grade ineffective warm-up drills is icing on the cake.

My intention is not to disparage the activities that you may use as class openers; some of them may have instructional value, but I challenge you to find anything that has more impact on reading achievement than independent reading.

We teachers have more than enough anecdotal evidence that the students who read the most are the best spellers, writers, and thinkers. No exercise gives more instructional bang for the buck than reading. The added bonus for us teachers? I have found that independent reading is also among the easiest instructional practices to plan, model, and implement.

When Students Are Done

My sixth-grade students are quirky, with one foot in childhood and one in adolescence. They still like teachers and are not too cool to show it. A flock of students are always eager to help me sort papers, run errands, or erase the board when they finish their class work for the day. Before I filled every stolen moment with invasive reading, students would ask me whether they could draw or do homework for other classes when they were done with their assignments and there were always a few students who disrupted others when they had finished their work. Their talking and classroom wanderings distracted the students who were still working and me while I was trying to assist others. Since I redesigned my class so that students use every free minute for independent reading, these disruptions have ceased. What should students do when they finish all of their assignments for the day? Student learning—reading, writing, and thinking—should continue from the first bell until the last. While we teachers decry the lack of time we have to teach, it seems that we misappropriate a great deal of what we do have on classroom chores and mindless work.

A popular practice in many classrooms is the creation and use of folders filled with extension activities and extra practice sheets—exercises designed to occupy students who finish class assignments quickly. I made them, too, in those early years, back when I was stuck in the mode of doing what everyone else around me did. Like warm-ups, these fun folders for the fast finishers had little instructional value other than drill and practice and took hours of time to plan and create. When my students asked me whether they could read their books instead of doing the folder assignments, I got the message.

When I took a closer look at those folders, it became clear to me that they were simply time wasters, busywork, and, in some ways, punishment for students who were capable. Students hate those supposedly fun folders. My husband, a self-proclaimed slacker in school, figured out that when he finished his assignments earlier than other students, his reward was more work. He began to work more and more slowly, stretching out assignments that he could easily have finished in order to avoid the extra work. I surely reject any activity that fosters underachievement in students! I got rid of the folders. And my students started reading. Invasive reading helps students meet their reading goals for the class, engages them in an enjoyable practice that contributes to their academic achievement, frees me to work with students that may need my help, and minimizes off-task behavior problems. I can tell when my students are done with their assignments by listening, not because my classroom becomes rowdy and loud but because it becomes quiet when every student is reading.

At a recent district curriculum-writing meeting, a colleague expressed her concern when I told her that I did not plan extra activities for my students to complete when they were finished with their class work: "Aren't you worried that they will rush through their work in order to get back to their books?" Amused by her shocked expression, I waited a beat, and answered, "Lord, I hope so!"

Reflecting on the habits of life readers, it is clear that this reading time matches what they do anyway. What do adult readers do when they finish their work for the day? They reward themselves by snuggling up with their books.

Picture Day

Only those who work in schools can fully appreciate what a big deal picture day is. My sixth-grade girls show up decked out in sweater sets, curled hair, and high-heeled shoes they will only have to abandon before they go to gym. The boys sport button-down shirts (covering the T-shirts they usually wear) and dangerous levels of hair gel to maintain their spikes. Getting 850 students through the picture line in less than three hours is a marvel of institutional machinery. My students may love my class, but ditching it to stand in line and chat with their friends for thirty minutes holds a powerful allure. In years past, I spent most of my time during picture day walking up and down the line, monitoring behavior and shushing my students. The students who had already had their pictures taken and were waiting for the rest of the class were the rowdiest. Not only was I frustrated by my students' behavior, but I was itchy about the class time I was losing.

Once again, the habits of the readers in my classroom and my own experience of carrying a book everywhere I go led me to the answer. The penny dropped one picture day when I found myself holding three books for my voracious readers while they had photographs taken. Reclaiming this waiting time as reading time, we take our books to picture day now. I hold students' books in a basket while they get their pictures taken, and then they grab them from me, sit against the wall, and read while waiting for the rest of the class. One year, my students were so accustomed to carrying their books with them to picture day and beyond that they insisted on posing with their books in the class yearbook picture that spring.

I know that the more time students spend reading each day, the more ingrained it becomes as a daily habit. Recognizing the success of my efforts to carve out more reading time for my students, I constantly look for other chances for them to read during unstructured moments. Endless time is lost during a school year in waiting for assemblies, riding buses, and standing in lines. I have commandeered this unstructured time for my students to read, and as a result, misbehavior at such times is almost nonexistent and my students rack up substantial reading time that they formerly spent talking, getting into trouble, or standing around being bored (see Figure 3.1). Might I add that those students who are experts at stalling during reading time in class cannot hide the fact that they are not reading when it is a ubiquitous activity in my classroom throughout the school day? If everyone else in the class is sitting against the wall, reading, while waiting for class pictures and a few students aren't, it becomes obvious quickly. By setting the expectation that reading is what we do, always, everywhere, it becomes the heart of a class's culture. Even the most resistant readers can't fight it if all of their friends comply.

Library Time

Ah, libraries. God, I love them—the rows and rows of books waiting for me, the comfy chairs beckoning me to linger and read. Full of what Virginia Woolf calls "sunk treasure," libraries offer wealth to

FIGURE 3.1: *Students read while waiting for their field-trip bus.*

any reader. One of my great joys is that I get to work every day in a building with a library in it.

In spite of the fact that we have an extensive classroom library of over two thousand books, I insist on taking my students to the school library on a regular basis—at least every two weeks, if not more often. Part of wearing a reader's clothes is learning how to navigate a library and feeling at home in one. Poring through the stacks alongside my students is a great opportunity for me to show them how to find books, expose them to a larger collection, and teach library etiquette.

Kim Gardner, my librarian friend, dubbed me the Pied Piper after watching a trail of students follow me through the library. She saw how hypnotized my students were while we looked at books and chose them together. Focusing their efforts on finding books and reading during library visits are not skills students always enter my class with, however. These behaviors must be modeled and explicitly taught. Many students see a trip to the library as yet another opportunity for free time or a chance to goof off with their friends and cluster in groups to chat under the guise of looking for books. Neither teachers nor librarians should spend classroom library visits monitoring behavior. Their time is better spent helping students find books to read. Library time should not be perceived as unstructured free time by students or, worse, lost instructional time by their teachers. I know middle school teachers who do not even take their students to the library because to them, it is a "waste of class time." If library visits are focused on choosing books and stealing time to read, there is no need to bark at students to find a book or shush them. Students rise to the level of their teacher's expectations, so make your expectations for library visits clear.

Setting Goals for Library Use

Setting the goals of reading and selecting books when my students go to the library happens on our first visit. My modeling starts with my giddiness as the first library day arrives. I begin mentioning to students that we are going to the library several days ahead of time and imagine with them the wonderful books we will find there. I post library days on our class Web site. I want students to pick up on the fact that I think library days are events to anticipate. On the big day, I always ask a student to remind me when it is a few minutes before our assigned library time, so that we can line up and get there promptly.

When we line up to go to the library, every student must have a book to return, renew, or read, or a plan to get one at the library. Because the main source of books for my students is our own classroom library, students may bring these books if they do not want to check out an additional book from the school library.

If students do not carry a book, then they will spend their time in the library looking for one. The goal is that everyone walks out of the library with a book to read. My students tease me, crying, "Not fair!" when they realize that by teaching two classes, I get double trips to the library on a single day.

When we get to the library, all students are purposeful. If they are checking out books, they immediately begin looking. Students who are not checking out books head to quiet corners and read. No one visits, no one clusters, and no one talks. OK, not exactly true . . . . A devoted tribe of followers accompanies me and chats while we roam the stacks, hunting and gathering books. I spend the entire visit helping students locate books, but I cannot contain my own excitement when I discover treasures I would like to read, too. My students are jealous of the teacher perks of library use—no fines, no due dates, and unlimited checkouts—all privileges I exploit fully.

Because I work with my students to find books and eliminate off-task library behavior, our librarian is free to check out books and assist students who need help with searching the library's online catalogue. When everyone has a book to read, we all sit and read until our library time ends or we leave the library and go back to class to read.

How Much Time Is It, Really?

Counting all the snippets of time I manage to gather in a typical school week, how much reading time do I really capture for my students? Replacing warm-ups with reading time and stealing as many stray moments as possible, I calculate, gains twenty to thirty minutes of reading per day. The Commission on Reading's touchstone report *Becoming a Nation of Readers* recommends that students engage in two hours of silent sustained reading per week (Anderson, Hiebert, Scott, and Wilkinson, 1985). Without giving up any instructional time, you could easily find two hours a week for your students. If you are willing to set aside a chunk of class time for independent reading as well, your students could be reading as much as four hours a week *in school*.

My students are now time stealers themselves, using otherwise wasted time in their daily routine to read. Paul reads at the bus stop in the mornings, and Daniel reads while waiting for his mom to pick him up from school. Alex reads at lunchtime, and Madison reads at recess while she sits under a tree. Once students catch the reading bug, they will go to great lengths to find time to read.

While I was greeting students in the hall one morning, Molly breathlessly ran up to me to share the creative way she was able to continue reading her latest mystery book, *The Ghost's Grave*, by Peg Kehret. "Mrs. Miller, you have had such an influence on me. Last night I read in the shower!"

Amused, I asked, "How were you able to read in the shower and keep the book dry?"

Other students gathered around us, not to look at the reading freak but to listen to Molly's advice so they could do it, too. "I was at the end of my book, and my mom was yelling for me to get in the shower. So I hung my arm out of the shower as far as possible so I could keep reading it."

Another student suggested, "Hey, I wonder if you could slide a Ziploc bag over a book to protect it while you read it in the shower!"

Although I am disinclined to recommend reading books in the shower, for the health of both the reader and the book, it is important to encourage young readers when they explore options for reading anywhere they can. Adult readers have mastered this art, reading in airports, while commuting, or in doctors' offices to alleviate boredom. Readers steal time to read.

Creating a Place for Reading

The time to read is any time: no apparatus, no appointment of time and place, is necessary. It is the only art which can be practised at any hour of the day or night, whenever the time and inclination comes, that is your time for reading; in joy or sorrow, health or illness.

—Holbrook Jackson

My husband, Don, carries a book with him everywhere. Even though I am a reader, too, it irritated me in the early years of our marriage when he would bring a book to Thanksgiving dinner at my mother's house or on trips to the grocery store. Once, he walked into a tree in the middle of a city sidewalk because he was reading as he moseyed home from work. I marvel at Don's ability to read anywhere, even in noisy crowds or standing up. After many jealous moments when we would find ourselves unexpectedly stuck somewhere, Don with his book and me without one, I started carrying a book everywhere I went, too. Don and I prefer to read our books curled up on the couch at home, but we do not need an ideal environment in order to snatch some reading time. With this kind of I-can-read-anywhere attitude, I'm not an advocate of the reading corner, as anyone who visits my class-room will quickly note.

Imagine a small room with twenty-nine sixth graders of various heights and sizes, an overflowing library of more than two thou-sand books, and all of the items a school requires a teacher to keep on hand—crisis tubs, file cabinets, and textbook ancillaries— and you have my classroom. I do not have the space to dedicate a corner for reading.

> *As you probably know, I read at my relative's house in Miami. I don't think they really cared, of course they might have been talking about me in Spanish, but I wouldn't know.*
>
> —**Michelle**

> *When we were at a rodeo and the main act was two little kids dancing around with ribbons and streamers and the rodeo contestants got ready, I just pulled out* Behind the Bedroom Wall *and finished it before the barrel racing.*—**Marilyn**

Jace, of book-frenzy fame, and his mom donated an old leather sofa to my classroom a few years ago when they bought a new one. After nominating several names and taking a class vote, my students christened it "Aunt Fanny" (see Figure 3.2). Poor Aunt Fanny is now crammed under the windowsill. We have a motley collection of beanbag chairs that I have scavenged over the years from donations and garage sales, which my students fall over constantly. We do have wonderful adjustable lighting—one of the perks of being at a new school. I keep the lights dimmed a little so that students can read without the harsh glare of fluorescence. I do not care where or how my students read in my room, only that they are reading. They may lie on the floor, take their shoes off, or remain at their desks. Why should it matter?

One morning, while dragging my students out of their books with my usual call, "Ladies and gentlemen, come to a stopping place," I noticed that Daniel, always one of the hardest to pull out of his book, was not heading back to his desk. I went looking for him. Daniel had wedged himself into a corner between the sofa and a bookcase, a self-created burrow where he could read in peace, out of the traffic flow.

Countless reading mavens emphasize in their books and workshops the importance of setting up a dedicated place for students to read. Rugs, cushions, lamps, bookcases—all should be deliberately and artfully placed to create a reading sanctuary. Rankling over the space limitations in my classroom, it frustrated me when I could not feng shui my furniture and the children into some sort of reading oasis. I was letting the gurus down and, probably, my students. I once mentioned to Ron, my principal, that I wanted to pull out all of the desks and drag in couches and coffee tables,

FIGURE 3.2: *Students read while sitting on Aunt Fanny.*

turning my room into a Barnes & Noble. He laughed and shook his head. He thought I was joking . . . .

As I often do when confronted with an ideal that I cannot seem to achieve, I stepped back to reconsider the true intent of the dedicated reading corner. As I see it, the reading area in a classroom is meant to serve two purposes: to send the message to students that reading is important by setting aside a prominent place for it in the room and to provide students with comfortable conditions in which to read by not confining them to institutionally mandated seating at desks under harsh lighting. Can we do this without the community rug and the floor lamps? Of course we can.

> *Have you ever tried reading upside down on the monkey bars? Let's just say that one didn't work out very well. The book fell and I lost my page, so I tried for it and I landed on my head. Not smart!* —**Brittany**

I have never seen a student who became a reader because of access to a beanbag chair. What do we hope to accomplish by designing a living room in which students can read? After all, don't we bemoan the fact that students don't read in their living room at home? If you have a quiet reading corner, by all means, use it. I support any classroom design that makes it less institutional and more inviting to students, but don't regret it if you don't have the resources or space for a dedicated reading area. Readers are remarkably ingenious and resourceful when it comes to finding a place to read.

In New York City, I saw a man on the subway hanging on to a strap with one hand while holding the book he was reading in the other—no cozy nook needed. I was instantly reminded of my husband, who power-reads books on the train while jamming to his iPod. I have students every year who read while walking down the hall (They seem to have some internal GPS that prevents them from walking into things!); riding the school bus; or sitting in a crowded, noisy lunchroom. A classroom atmosphere that promotes reading does not come from the furniture and its placement as much as it comes from the teacher's expectation that students will read. Accepting this, I know that my entire room is a reading haven, a place where students can read in comfort and where reading doesn't require a dedicated area to take center stage every single day. We must send the message that any place can be the right place for reading, whether it's on the subway or in an out-of-the-way corner. Students needn't

Unusual Places to Read

by Mrs. Miller's class

shower
empty bathtub
under the bed
grocery store
closet
roof
stairs
on top of brick mailbox
hedges and trees
trampoline
using dog as a pillow
in the open trunk of a car

wait for perfect conditions to start reading. The time is now, and the place is here.

Quiet, Please (Except Maybe This Teacher)

I insist on quiet during reading workshop time; I think this is because I need quiet to read and I know that quite a few of my students cannot fall into a book without limits on noise. A few years ago, while I wandered the classroom looking for students who needed help finding a book, I noticed four boys, Grant, Tien, Joel, and Brett, whom I had nicknamed the "*Eragon* Posse" after their shared love for Christopher Paolini's book (now a trilogy), whispering in the back corner of the room. "You boys had better be talking about literature back there!" I barked as I ambled over to them, determined to squelch any nonreading behavior. Assuring me that they were on task, Grant sheepishly raised his head and said, "We are!"

Embarrassed by that episode, I am now more likely to sidle up to whispering students to determine whether they are talking about books before I shush them. Building a trusting relationship with students is easier when you expect them to do the right thing instead of assuming that they are not. During independent reading time, the chattier students share recommendations or read exciting parts of their books to each other. They have a lot of time to talk to each other during the day, but this is their time to talk about reading. They enjoy the opportunity to chat with each other about what they are reading and what they are getting from their books.

Honestly, I am the person most likely to make noise during reading workshop time. I am not quiet by nature and find it hard to whisper during conferences. I often get so excited about the books I am discussing with a student that I shout queries to the rest of the class: "Hey, who has read *Tangerine*? Would you recommend it to Jonathan? He needs a realistic fiction suggestion!"

Limiting talking among students during independent reading time reinforces to students the importance of respecting classmates who need a quiet environment in order to read, but I recognize that there are legitimate moments of natural dialogue that support reading, too—even if the teacher is the one talking!

Walking by Michelle's table one morning, I stopped to talk to her about the upcoming movie *Inkheart*, which is based on one of our favorite books. Michelle agreed that fans of the book would love to see the movie. We began to talk about our hopes for the film and which parts of Cornelia Funke's ode to the power of books we most looked forward to seeing on screen. My enthusiastic conversation with Michelle not only pulled her out of the book she was reading but also drew in the other five students sitting around her. I can justify distracting students in this way because I know that talking about books is vital to a reading community, and these conversations develop relationships among my students and me.

CHAPTER 4

Reading Freedom

Any book that helps a child to form a habit of reading,
to make reading one of his deep and continuing needs,
is good for him.

—Richard McKenna

Reading is what I do now, especially when I'm bored. I know I will do it. I just know.

—Brandon

STANDING AT THE FRONT of my classroom, marker in hand, chart paper at the ready, I am leading a discussion with my new students about how readers choose books for themselves. In spite of our book frenzy the day before, my students have not yet accepted that this class will be different, that their reading choices and honesty will drive everything that we do. Students raise their hands to give me the answers they think I want to hear:

"I look at the cover and the title."

"I read the summary on the back of the book."

We stop and discuss the differences between a summary, which describes the plot of a book in detail, including the resolution; a teaser, which gives you a taste of the book without revealing the entire plot; and a blurb, which is a reviewer's reaction to the book. After exploring this tangent, students continue to tell me how they choose their books:

"I look for an author who I have read before."

"I like to read series that I can follow."

"I get recommendations from my sister. She was in sixth grade last year."

We add friends, family members, librarians, and teachers to the pool of people from whom we get recommendations.

Another student offers, "I pick books from the display at the bookstore."

I doubt that most of my students choose their books from a nifty display at Barnes & Noble. Some of them have probably never chosen a book on their own. They are feeling me out. Their comments sound like questions, waiting for confirmation of their predictable replies. If I accept their pat answers, ones that students who do not even read could provide, then they will know that my pep talk about honesty is all talk. Instead, I challenge them with questions they might never expect me to ask.

I am the teacher, and there are aspects to choosing books that these new students do not think they can admit to me or verbalize because they reveal reading habits that are viewed as "cheating" or "not really reading," so I ask, "Who has chosen a book because it is short? Who has chosen a book to read by checking how long it is?" With sheepish smiles, most of the people in the room (including me) raise a hand. "Come on, guys, I do this, too. It's OK for you to admit it. Sometimes I do not have the energy or time to commit to a long book, but I want to read something." We travel down this tangent for several minutes, discussing the best short books we have read, and make a list of those, too.

With this wall down, we discuss the methods students use to choose books that they are reluctant to admit. Many of the students who do not see themselves as good readers did not realize before this class discussion that *all* readers "cheat."

> I have been admonished by parents and fellow teachers because I let children read a book more than once. My most treasured books have been read many times by me and each time I discover something different. Books are multilayered; one reading is not enough and this is known only to those who truly read.—comment from JoAnn on blog entry "How to Kindle Reading" in "The Book Whisperer," December 13, 2007

We add the following to our list of book selection techniques:

"I like to read some books over and over."

"I read the ending first, and then if I like it, I read the whole book."

"I read the first paragraph, and if it doesn't grab me, I put it down."

"I read books that are easy."

"I read fantasy books. My mom tries to get me to read something else, but I just don't like her books."

The students are into it now. Their hidden opinions are flying out of their mouths from every corner of the room, and as I struggle to get all of their comments onto the chart paper, Brian grumbles, "Books are boring."

The laughter and comments from around the room screech to a halt. Oops, are we supposed to admit to the teacher that we find books boring? The other students edge their desks away from Brian, fearing the inevitable lightning strike. The furtive glances toward Brian tell me that all of the walls are not down yet. The students look at me to see how I am going to deal with Brian's comment, so here goes.

I turn toward Brian, knowing that all of the children need to hear what I say next: "I am so glad that you said that! Some books are boring." I share my experiences with the book *Mayflower* by Nathaniel Philbrick, which I read recently with my book group. "I read a hundred pages of that book, and I still couldn't get into it. I tried. Everyone was raving about the book, and it was on all of the 'best books' lists this year, but I got bored with the Indian Wars and the long lists of people and places. I finally abandoned it. When I went to my book club meeting this month, I was relieved to find out that some of the other members felt the same way I did!"

My testimonial reopens the floodgates. We launch into a discussion of what to do when a book gets boring, and I give my students outright permission to abandon books that are not working for them. Readers choose what to read and when to stop reading a book that doesn't live up to its potential. I never want my students to feel that they are roped into a book just because they have started reading it. Getting a feel for the genres and reading level that is the best fit requires reading several books, including some false starts. "Hey, there is always another book waiting. If you are reading a book that is too hard or too boring to keep going, abandon it, and get another one. The important thing is not to let a bad book choice slow down your momentum for reading. Readers do this all of the time. Don't feel that you have to stick with a book just because you started it."

Courtney sings out a modified version of Dory's mantra from the Disney movie *Finding Nemo*, "Just keep reading. Just keep reading." Everyone laughs, and I can tell that they are beginning to relax.

Bongani asks, "What books are we going to read in class this year? We read *Johnny Tremain* last year."

I ignore the groans from the other students who must have been in Bongani's fifth-grade class and reply, "I don't know. What would you like to read? Are there books that we should share as a class together? What are some books that you would suggest? Let me know if you have books that you think we would enjoy, and we can discuss them. I have some books that I like to read aloud to my classes every year because everyone likes them, but I am open to your ideas, too."

I believe that students should be empowered to make as many book choices as possible, including the books we read together. The idea of students clamoring to read favorite books feeds into my goal for getting them excited about reading. By valuing their opinions, even about the books we share as a class, I let them know that their preferences are as important as mine.

A few days later, I share with my students "The Rights of the Reader," by French author Daniel Pennac. This list is available on the Web as a download-able poster with funky Quentin Blake illustrations at http://www.walker.co.uk/bookshelf/the-rights-of-the-reader-poster.aspx. As a reader, you will, no doubt, recognize these rights yourself.

I caution you not to hang this poster in your classroom; it will become wallpaper that students will cease to see after a few months. Even though I teach many of the same lessons to students year after year, I resist the urge to make posters out of these lessons and then reuse them, because I do not want students to think that their opinions are not original or that I can predict what they will say. Each class is different, and it is important for my students to see their ideas and their words—not someone else's—hanging on our walls as advice for all readers to follow. First, have the dialogue with your students about their own reading habits, and then provide Pennac's list of rights later as an endorsement of what they have already shared.

THE RIGHTS OF THE READER

BY DANIEL PENNAC
1. The right to not read.
2. The right to skip pages.
3. The right to not finish.
4. The right to reread.
5. The right to read anything.
6. The right to escapism.
7. The right to read anywhere.
8. The right to browse.
9. The right to read out loud.
10. The right not to defend your tastes.

Source: Pennac, 2006.

Reading Plans

In addition to rereading favorites, stealing time to read, and abandoning books that are not working for them, readers look ahead to their next book. Reading the Newbery medalists each year has been part of my reading plan since I was a fourth grader. Now I devour lists and reviews from *Booklist* magazine and Amazon. When

I realized that I had covered the back of every checkbook pad and receipt in my wallet with book titles and authors' names—constantly jotted down during chats with my reading friends—I started keeping a journal in my purse. Beginning a new journal each year, I scrawl down every recommendation I get and use these notes when I buy books or go to the library. This year's model is a three-by-five-inch, pocket-sized Moleskine notebook. The acid-free paper keeps my book lists from smudging and fading, and using the same brand of notebook that Hemingway supposedly used makes me feel literary.

An entire bookcase in my living room is filled with books I am planning to read—books I have borrowed, checked out from the library, or purchased. Laughingly referred to as "Miller Mountain," this avalanche of books never gets smaller and guarantees that I will never run out of books to read. This overwhelming pile is often my excuse to students when I have not returned a book loan from them in a timely fashion, but it is also a reminder to them that I am always planning to read another book.

Unaccustomed to making their own reading choices at first, quite a few students, especially those who do not see themselves as readers, do not make plans for future reading. In school, their teacher tells them what books they will read and when. These students do not have much knowledge about the types of books available and few positive experiences with books that might inform their reading choices. They need a place to start. To provide scaffolding that will help them develop their own plans, I provide students with an approach for the reading they will do in my class.

Reading Requirements: Why Forty Books?

That I require students to read forty books may seem shocking when you are a student who has not read more than a book or two a year, but this hefty requirement prevents students from negotiating with me about whether they will read much. Any teacher who expects students to read forty books is not going to accept a book or two! If I expected less, they would read less, or they would wait until later in the school year to start.

Ten books or twenty books are not enough to instill a love of reading in students. They must choose and read many books for themselves in order to catch the reading bug. By setting the requirement as high as I do, I ensure that students must have a book going constantly. Without the need to read a book every single day to stay on top of my requirement, students would read as little as they could. They might not internalize independent reading habits if my requirement expected less from them. I know this approach works because I have never had a student who reached the forty-book mark stop there. Students continue to read even after the requirement is met.

Some students are not confident that they will be able to reach this goal, but I assure them that they can. I am encouraging and supportive but firm, telling them, "Let's pick a book and get started. Lots of students, all kinds of readers, have done this. I know that you can do it, too." I have seen students read an amazing number of books through the years, and I know that my reading requirement eventually becomes a non-issue for most of them. Brittany looks back on her accomplishments during the year: "When I learned that we had to read forty books this year, I flipped out. I had only read two books last year. I wanted to *faint*. As I made my way through the requirements, I slowly realized how much reading potential I had."

When my students ask me what will happen to them if they do not read forty books, I am vague. Failure is not an option, so why talk

> *I think that the reading requirements are quite understandable because if we didn't have a requirement, then people like me would read one book for the whole year.* **—Jon**

about it? I think it is horrible that reading, for them, is an act worth doing only to pass a class. In reality, there is no negative consequence for falling short of this goal. After all, if a student reads twenty-two books in a school year (the fewest any of my students has ever read), who could take issue with that?

Over the years, my class reading requirement has morphed into an amalgam of suggested genres from my training-wheels book on reading workshops, Fountas and Pinnell's *Guiding Readers and Writers (Grades 3–6)*; the goals of Texas's sixth-grade language arts and social studies curriculum; and the types of books I noticed that my students like to read.

My students select from a range of materials, including poetry, fiction, and nonfiction. Poetry anthologies, nonfiction texts (including biographies and informational texts), and traditional literature selections (including mythology, folktales, and legends) are generally shorter books of less than a hundred pages. Fiction titles (fantasy, science fiction, historical fiction, and realistic fiction) are chapter-book length. I set a specific number of books that students must read in each genre, but I also allow them to choose nine from any genre to complete the forty-book total. The number of books set for each genre is not carved in stone; in fact, I change it from year to year. When my students asked me to create a mystery category, I did so. When my district curriculum set guidelines for a poetry unit, I added more books to my poetry requirements.

FORTY-BOOK REQUIREMENT

Poetry anthologies 5

Traditional literature 5

Realistic fiction 5

Historical fiction 2

Fantasy 4

Science fiction 2

Mystery 2

Informational 4

Biography, autobiography,
   memoir 2

Chapter-book choice 9

This reading requirement exposes students to a variety of books and genres so that they can explore books they might not ordinarily read and develop an understanding of the literary elements, text features, and text structures of most books. Furthermore, a wide range of genres enables me to design instruction around my district's mandates and state standards and still give my students the chance to select their own books in order to complete assignments that are already part of the curriculum. Students can use a wide range of books to access the broad concepts and themes they are expected to learn. As a language arts and social studies teacher, I prefer to integrate these subjects by layering reading and writing activities within Texas's sixth-grade world cultures curriculum.

> *I like that I have to read a variety of books because otherwise, I wouldn't.*
> **—Rachel**

For each region we investigate, I gather books on the history, people, and fiction indigenous to that part of the world. When we study the history and culture of Europe, students read folk and fairy tales from the Brothers Grimm, Charles Perrault, and Hans Christian Andersen. They try their hand at writing traditional literature by mirroring the motifs and themes of the classics we read. When we explore the culture of Japan, we read and write haiku poetry.

I have learned that students hunger for more information, beyond what their social studies textbook offers if we go the extra mile to provide it. To this end, I line the marker rail under our classroom white boards with regional text sets. This gives students an additional opportunity to read and research regional cultures and to become engrossed in regional literature. It also encourages students to explore and pursue their particular cultural interests. All of it ties back to our social studies discussions, furthering inquiry.

It's About Reading, Not Requirements

Requiring students to read a certain number of books has led to some unanticipated challenges. The first year I set such a reading goal, I noticed that my developing and dormant readers selected the shortest books they could find to get the job done. Expecting such a large number of books was an issue for a few of my underground readers, too. How would they ever read forty books when the books they loved the most were epic tomes with a staggering number of pages? I solved this problem by letting students count any book over 350 pages as two books toward the requirement. This prevents students from choosing books simply because they are short, acknowledges the preferences of students who like to read hefty volumes, and frees all of them to read whatever books they want—short or long.

Bongani recalls his reaction when he heard he had to read so many books: "When you said forty books my heart stopped and I blacked out for several seconds. Then it struck me. Forty Dr. Seuss books for forty days! When you told us about the genre requirements, I immediately said, 'I am going to bomb this class.'"

During a conference with Paul, he admitted that he began the year by picking the shortest books he could find from each genre so that he would meet the class goals, but he wasn't doing that anymore. When I asked him what brought on this change, he told me that he had already read seventeen books by the end of the first nine weeks of school and he knew he would reach the forty mark by June. "I am going to read whatever I want, and just let it happen," he told me. This tells me that Paul has gained reading confidence. Because he had never been given the freedom to choose his own books, extensive time to read them, or high expectations from a teacher, he did not believe he could do it. A few weeks in our

> *This year I learned that I can actually enjoy realistic fiction! I used to read only fantasy, but now I read a lot more.*   **—Alex**

class has changed Paul's view of himself as a reader and what he can accomplish.

Does expecting every student to read the genre requirements always work? No, it doesn't. Every year, I have students who are so attached to their beloved genres that, in fact, they do not meet the genre requirements. One year, Tommy, a staunch fantasy fan, read sixty-five fantasy and science fiction books but avoided almost every other genre of book. Like Randy, his identity as a reader was strong. He knew what he liked, and he enjoyed the freedom to read whatever he wanted. I tried to entice him with other books, but if he showed no interest, I did not press the issue. I got it this time, and left Tommy to read what he wanted. Is there anyone who doubts that Tommy is a reader because he did not complete my structured genre requirements?

Reading widely expands a reader's knowledge of a variety of texts, but there are benefits to reading deeply in one genre, too. Talking with Tommy for two minutes revealed the depth of knowledge he had acquired about fortresses, armaments, mythology, and medieval history from all of those fantasy books. He also understood complex literary ideas like tone, allegory, and character archetypes right away when I taught them, having already discovered multiple examples from his books.

> *I like having a wide selection because I am a very picky reader and I can't force myself through a book I don't like. I would much rather choose a book than be assigned one!*
> **—Molly**

Meeting Students Where They Are

Madison did not meet her requirements, either. She was neither an enthusiastic nor a fast reader when she came to our class, and she did not find much joy in reading. With encouragement and lots of recommendations from her classmates and me, Madison read twenty-six books in sixth grade. She read more books that year than she had read on her own since starting school, a monumental achievement. Madison's preferences in books mirrored her favorite topics. She enjoyed realistic fiction about teen issues like popularity and dating. Without a community of readers to support her and the expectation of daily reading, Madison most likely will never read this much again.

Students who enjoy the social aspects of school, like Madison, read when it is required to participate in the culture of a class, but may not do so when the classroom climate changes. This point is particularly relevant in middle school, when students' behavior is dictated by what their peers value. Madison read because all of her friends in class did. Don't overlook the peer pressure and the need to belong that all adolescents succumb to as a powerful force in motivating students to read. I have seen many students pick up a book because it was recommended by a friend when they might not do so otherwise.

I refuse to take the control of students' reading back from them, even when they don't want it. Take Brandon as an example. The first two days of school, Brandon broke down and told me that he was never going to be able to read all of the books I expected him to because he hated to read and was not a good reader. He reluctantly chose *Well-Wished*, by Franny Billingsley, because a girl he liked in class was reading it. I would never have recommended this book to an active, sporty boy like Brandon. The readers who seemed to love this book were dreamy, fantasy-loving girls. Predictably, Brandon labored through this book for almost a month. At first, I cheerily asked Brandon how it was going. He would mumble that it was going OK, but I knew he wasn't in love with the book and he wasn't reading it very much.

I begged Brandon to abandon the book and choose another one, but I realized that this is exactly what Brandon was trying to avoid. Abandoning *Well-Wished* would mean he had to choose another book, and he did not want another book; he did not want *any* book. I think Brandon hoped I would give up, but he underestimated me and himself. I am sure that Brandon had been able to wear down teachers before me, managing to skirt the reading issue altogether.

My new tactic was to show Brandon stacks of books that he might enjoy more—books about boys having adventures. I simply kept plying him with books, stacks and stacks of books. We still talked about books at every conference, but now we talked about books Brandon might read instead of the one he wasn't reading. He finally gave in one day and chose *Hatchet*, by Gary Paulsen. Brandon read the first half of *Hatchet* begrudgingly, but he fell in love with it and sped through the last fifty pages. He proudly announced it to me when he was on the last chapter and then asked, "Do you have any of the other *Hatchet* books?" Now he is plowing through all of the Brian stories (God bless the prolific Gary Paulsen!) and planning camping trips—a Paulsen-inspired interest—with his family.

By refusing to take responsibility for Brandon reading or not reading, I forced him to take it. Reading was previously an act that the teacher controlled for him, and therefore, in his mind, failing to read was not his fault.

My goal for all of my students is for them to discover that they can be readers, but some of them struggle with going from no reading to a great deal of reading in one school year. It is important to celebrate milestones with students and focus on their reading successes, not their failure to meet requirements, which only serves to discourage students. Instead, I encourage and ask questions: "Did you read more than you thought you would?" "How many books did you read last year?" "Wow, look at how many more you read this year! Did you read books that you enjoyed?" "What surprised you about that?" When a student like Grant tells me that he had read one book in his entire life and that this year he had read twenty-three by March, how can I do anything other than celebrate and encourage him?

Validating Reading Choices

Another characteristic of readers is that we read for pure escapism sometimes. How many adolescent readers are reading books that adults deem to be of limited nutritional value as part of their reading diet? I need only look at what my own students are reading to learn everything I need to know. Andrew, who is not an avid reader, is currently absorbed in the book series that follows the story arc of his favorite video game, Halo. Bryce is reading an anthology of collected *Star Wars* stories. Lauren and Patty cannot get enough manga, Japanese comic books. And Tiffany is recommending Caroline Cooney's mystery *The Face on the Milk Carton* to all of her friends. None of these books would appear on a list of best books for young readers, but my students love to read them. No matter what books I try to provide for my students via our class library or recommend for them to read, I need to acknowledge some of their less-than-highbrow choices in reading material, too.

Books that are widely read are not always the books by the most esteemed authors or with the best reviews. Similarly, many of the books that are touted as works of great literary value are not read by many readers. Readers travel through both worlds, that of high art and that of popular culture. I believe that every American should read the Pulitzer Prize winner *To Kill a Mockingbird*, but I think they should also read Stephen King's cult classic *The Shining*. The books I choose to read with students, use in my teaching, or offer in my library may be different books than the ones I would wholeheartedly embrace for students' reading. By allowing and encouraging students to read what they want, I also endorse their culture and their interests—something we do not do enough in school.

Lucy Calkins's words from *The Art of Teaching Writing* remind us, "Our . . . workshop will not feel alive and significant if our students sit through it bored and uninvolved, waiting for the bell to ring and life to begin." Teachers lose credibility with students when they ignore the cultural trends and issues that interest them and instead design classroom reading instruction around books that are "good for you." There is a certain amount of disdain from teachers in regard to popular fiction for children because some of those books are mind candy, but I'd bet that some of those teachers go home and read escapist books like *Shopaholic* or a James Patterson thriller and never make the connection. Are we teaching books or teaching readers? I would rather have my students read books of questionable literary value than not read at all. Once students find at least one book they like and receive approval for reading books of their own choice, it is easier to move them toward books you suggest.

Take Mary, for example. She was not a big reader when she came to my class. She had read only one book that she really enjoyed, *The Day My Butt Went Psycho*, by Andy Griffiths. This book, the first in a trilogy, follows a small-town teenager whose backside and those of his fellow townspeople reveal themselves as an alien race of beings intent on world domination. Yes, they are from the planet Uranus. Mary suggested the book to me and offered to loan me her much-read copy. Setting aside my teacher hat and addressing the issue reader to reader, I did what readers do when someone recommends a book with such enthusiasm; I took the book and read it. Filled with gross body humor, awful puns, and an outrageous plotline, if this book added to Mary's vocabulary, they were probably words she didn't need to know.

What really mattered was that it meant everything to Mary that I had read this book and we were able to laugh about it for the entire year. Because I trusted and validated her as a reader, Mary trusted herself. From then on, she took many of my recommendations for more inspiring reading material. She moved on to more sophisticated novels and developed a love for historical fiction. By the time she left my class, Mary's favorite book of all time was *Girl in Blue*, by Ann Rinaldi, a novel about a girl who disguises herself as a boy in order to fight in the Civil War. A lot of students who start out reading books like *The Day My Butt Went Psycho* because they are immature as readers, do not have much experience in choosing books for themselves, or have not had much guidance. Most will branch out and broaden their repertoire of books with support from a more experienced reader. This is where you, the teacher, come in. What we must do is give our approval when students make their own reading choices, no matter what books they choose, because this is far preferable to their deciding not to read at all.

Especially with boys, I think letting them read books that are provocative or borderline appropriate, such as Robert Cormier's controversial *The Chocolate War* and *The Rag and Bone Shop* or Christopher Paul Curtis's shocking *Bucking the Sarge*, is motivating. What draws middle school and high school boys to the edgy themes of certain movies and video games, the visceral imagery, the suggestive scenes, the subversive tone can be found in young adult books; they just don't know it. One year, I had a whole group of boys who passed around *The Chocolate War* because they couldn't believe that a book could explore bullying and the teenage boy's experience in such a raw, honest way.

Teachers and parents often scorn the type of reading that boys most enjoy. Who cares if they want to read a book with bathroom humor or car crashes? Why should these boys read at all if they can never find their interests or relatable characters in the books adults steer them toward? I want to show the boys in my class that they can find themselves in books and can make reading an avenue for pursuing the topics that consume their attention.

Introducing Authors Through Read-Alouds

I teach sixth graders, so many of the books I read aloud to them are particular to this age and their concerns about moving into middle school. The first book I read aloud every year is *Tripping Over the Lunch Lady*, edited by Nancy Mercado, an anthology of school stories by popular authors. The stories cover a range of topics of interest to my students—being the new kid, having dyslexia, and the challenges of working with a group of strangers to complete a class project. We also share-read (I read and students follow along in their own copy) *The Sixth Grade Nickname Game*, by Gordon Korman, a favorite author year in and year out. No need to explain why I choose this realistic story about a group of sixth graders who are not the best readers but manage to ace the state reading exam by power-reading tons of books.

The memoirs of Gary Paulsen are also a consistent favorite. Paulsen's novels—like the survival classic *Hatchet*—are superb, but his personal memoirs, including his own survival tale *Guts*; the memorial to his beloved dogs, *My Life in Dog Years*; and the tales of his extreme stunts as a teenager, *How Angel Peterson Got His Name*, are annual hits. Because students' limited encounters with biographies and autobiographies usually start with a research assignment, they come into my class thinking that these types of books are dry time lines recounting the accomplishments of dead heroes. Paulsen's personal adventures can broaden a student's appreciation for reading about the lives of other people.

By reading these selections and others with my students early in the year, I expose them to about fifteen widely published fiction authors who are popular and interesting to young readers. These shared reading experiences enable me to make recommendations by connecting new books by the same authors to the stories we have enjoyed as a class. The following list of read-aloud favorites includes a range of titles from popular authors and genres for use with your class. The suggested age range for elementary titles is third through fifth grades; for intermediate titles, it is sixth through eighth grades. Elementary titles may also be a good fit for intermediate grades, and intermediate titles may work in elementary grades, depending on the needs or interests of your particular group

READ-ALOUD FAVORITES

Fiction

ELEMENTARY

Each Little Bird That Sings, by Deborah
    Wiles

The Sixth Grade Nickname Game, by
    Gordon Korman

The SOS Files, by Betsy Byars

The Word Eater, by Mary Amato

INTERMEDIATE

The Beasties, by William Sleator

The Underneath, by Kathi Appelt

The Schwa Was Here, by Neal
    Shusterman

Seedfolks, by Paul Fleischman

The Lightning Thief, by Rick Riordan

Memoirs

ELEMENTARY

Guts, by Gary Paulsen

Knots in My Yo-Yo String, by Jerry
    Spinelli

The Tarantula in My Purse, by Jean
    Craighead George

INTERMEDIATE

My Life in Dog Years, by Gary Paulsen

Small Steps: The Year I Got Polio, by Peg
    Kehret

How Angel Peterson Got His Name, by Gary
    Paulsen

of students. You may have your personal read-aloud favorites, but remember that my purpose for reading these books is to share several high-interest books with students as an introduction to authors who have written many other books that students can read on their own.

Building Background for Genre

As part of their education as readers, it is necessary for students to learn the common language that readers speak when discussing and investigating books. I frame instruction and discussions all year long around genre, the formal categorization of books. Some students are not familiar with the term, but they understand the difference between fiction and nonfiction and that books can share character types, plotlines, and settings. These story elements have been covered in classes before, but I am expected to revisit them, according to state standards.

Rather than force students to endure a boring rehash of information that they have learned previously, I use what students already know to build an understanding of how these elements differ across genres and how characterization, plot, and setting are used to classify books. Through class discussions, we develop guidelines for identifying nonfiction, too, exploring what types of information are provided by biographies or informational books, as well as text features and formats. Because most of my sixth graders have yet to be introduced to memoir, I find that this is a good time to introduce it; I define a memoir as an autobiography that focuses on a specific period in the author's life. Poetry I save for last because it does not clearly share the structure of other genres and has its own unique elements. I start our investigation of genre the same way each year because that allows me to assess students' prior knowledge of literary concepts and, at the same time, lay a foundation for future reading based on genre requirements. I need to get a feel for what students already know before we can move forward.

Genre Sets the Stage

With a pile of books in my hand and a grin on my face—a sight that will become all too common to my students as the year progresses—I call out to them, "Ladies and gentlemen, get out your genre notes so that we can talk about fantasy." Students pull out their genre notes, where they record the characteristics of each genre as we explore it, and find the heading for the fantasy section. "Keeping in mind our conversations about characters, what do we already know about the characters in fantasy books?"

One student claims, "Well, most characters in fantasy books are wizards or witches like Harry Potter."

"I agree that if a book has a wizard or magic user in it, then it has to be fantasy, but do *all* fantasy books have these kinds of characters? Can anyone give me an example of a book that doesn't have a wizard in it, but is still fantasy?"

Several students provide examples of books with realistic settings and characters that contain magical events, such as *Tuck Everlasting* and *The Word Eater*. This leads to another heated discussion about whether books that have talking animals in them, such as *Charlotte's*

Web and *Redwall*, are fantasy or not. We decide they are. I dash off as many of my students' ideas as I can onto chart paper, all the while urging students to avoid generalizations by staying away from words such as *all* and *every* when making their suggestions. Because twelve-year-olds can still be fairly literal, I explain that there are subtle distinctions even within a genre.

I remind them, "Honestly, fantasy books could have any type of character you could imagine, including everyday people, but what we are looking for are character types that cannot occur in any genre *but* fantasy."

We eventually decide on some broad character types that earmark a book as fantasy: magic users, talking animals, and mythical creatures. During this conversation, we have discussed scores of books and even some movies in order to provide evidence that supports our opinions. Students may not have had enough reading experiences to illustrate the genre discussion with book examples, but they know stories. Basic story grammar is found in the movies and television shows they watch, too. Encouraging students to give examples based on any knowledge they have, not just from books, prevents the avid readers from dominating all of the early discussions we have about books and shows students that I value what they do understand. This practice provides yet another inroad to meeting students where they are.

Moving on to discuss the settings and plotlines common to fantasy novels, we add these characteristics to the list. Over the course of two weeks or so, we investigate all of the genres in our class library and create lists of the elements of each. We also review characterization, plot, setting, text structure, and figurative language. We talk about how time travel by magic determines that a book is fantasy, whereas time travel by means of advanced technology renders it science fiction. We debate whether historical events have to be the center of a plot to make a book historical fiction. New terms such as *anthology* and *novella* arise naturally from these conversations, too. We talk and talk about books.

Through these conversations, I am able to assess my students' prior knowledge and reading experiences. Melissa's notes from this series of class discussions show how these conversations shaped her understanding of the characteristics of each genre (see Figure 4.1).

While we create definitions, we also look at stacks of books to determine whether students' knowledge of the characteristics of each genre can help them determine a book's genre when previewing it. Understanding the basic structure and plotlines of different genres helps students choose books and make predictions while reading. Students without a reading identity, who do not know enough about books to know what they might like to read, gain a greater understanding of the kinds of books available to them, too.

Identifying Books in Each Genre

In order to move our discussions of the characteristics of individual genres beyond a merely academic exercise, I expect students to be able to apply what they have learned to books they may not have read. Our classroom library is organized by genre, and I want to know whether students can use their understanding of genre to select books in our library and make assumptions about what each offers to readers.

A few weeks into our unit on genre, students walk in the door to find several unmarked tubs from our class library waiting for them at every desk group.

I lead them to today's topic by sharing one tub of books with them. "In this tub, I have several books that are from the same genre. As I read to you the teasers on the backs of these books, use your notes and our class discussions to determine which genre you think this tub contains."

Melissa

Characteristics of Genre Notes

Genre is a French word meaning type or kind. We use genres as a system to classify
books by their common characteristics.

Poetry
1. Definition-shortened form of writing
2. Figurative language-metaphors, similes, personification
3. Author's expression of feelings, opinions
4. May follow a form/structure

Traditional Literature
1. Definition-stories passed ~~oto~~ down for generations by
2. oral storytelling
3. myth, legends, folk tales, fairy tales, nursery rhymes, talls tales
4. foundation for fantasy

Fantasy
1. Characters: talking animals, mythical creature, magic users
2. Setting: often medieval, time travel (magic)
3. Plot: herds journey/quest, often good vs. evil.
4. _____

Science Fiction
1. Characters: mutants, robot, aliens, "mad" scientist, talking computer
2. Setting: advanced tech-cities, spaceships, other solar system, past
3. galaxy, time travel (technology)
4. Plot: alien atacks/visits, time traveling, technology important, experiments "gone wrong"

Realistic Fiction
1. Characters: every people doing everyday things
2. Setting: modern time, realistic place
3. Plot: realistic events
4. _____

FIGURE 4.1: *A Student's Notes on the Characteristics of Genres*
Source: Melissa, grade 6.

Melissa

Historical Fiction

1. Characters: famous historical people
2. Setting: pre 1970, could be historical/important sites
3. Plot: authentic historical events, average or significant
4. people

Mystery

1. Characters: detective, investigators, ~~police officer~~, spies
2. Setting: could be crime scene, detective agency, often creepy house
3. Plot: crime or mysterious event + clues = solution.
4.

Biography/ Autobiography/ Memoir

1. Biography-story of someones life, written by someone eles
2. Autobiography-story of someones life, written by themselves
3. Memoir - a short account of the author's experiences written by themselves
4.

Informational

1. purpose - providedes information on a wide range of topics
2. nonfiction
3. science, ~~history~~, crafts, sports, articales, Soeail Studies,
4.

nonfictional
Inform you on things you want to be informed on

After students determine that the books in my tub are realistic fiction because the events, settings, and characters seem plausible to them, I direct their attention to the tubs on their desks: "Now, I want you to work with your table groups. Use your knowledge of genre characteristics to identify the genre of the books in the tubs on your desks."

Engrossed in note taking and previewing books, students dig into the tubs at their desks. Two girls in the back of the room wave me over to serve as mediator. Their group is at an impasse and cannot agree on which genre their plastic tub contains.

"We think the books are historical fiction because the back covers of different books mention historical things like Ben Franklin and World War II, but Stacy and I do not think that the boy in this one was a real person from history."

Cody, a member of the group, chimes in: "Ben Franklin was a real person, and World War II really happened. These books are informational."

I guide them back to our class discussions: "Well, what is the difference between an informational book and one that is historical fiction?"

Cody asserts, "We don't know if this boy was made up; he could be real."

I urge the group to use their genre notes as a checklist to see whether all of the books in the tub have elements of historical fiction or elements of informational books. Determining whether the events and people in every book are real is the deciding factor here.

Cody lost the battle; the girls were right. *Foster's War*, by Carolyn Reeder, clinched it. After deciding that despite the World War II setting and plot events revealed in the teaser, the protagonist, Foster Simmons, was a fictional character, Cody grudgingly agreed that the tub they were previewing was historical fiction. He did not really lose. I saw him ease the book into his desk later.

This hands-on session allows students not only to reinforce what they have learned about genre by applying what they have learned to real books but also to preview a lot of books and become acquainted with the layout of the class library. Following this exercise, I always notice how many books disappear out of tubs and into desks, to be checked out later. As the culmination of our genre unit, I give the students a practical exam. Each student is given four books, and he or she must identify the genre of each. I rarely find a student who can't identify the genre of most of the books.

In a few short weeks, the groundwork has been laid for our reading year. Students have settled into the routine of reading each day and have a reading plan based on broad requirements for self-selected materials. I have built students' background knowledge of a wide range of genres and authors, and they know that I value their book choices and celebrate any reading they do. What I do and what they do wraps around this structure and provides a base for the reading, writing, and response activities at the next level of our workshop.

On the Same Page: Keeping a Reader's Notebook

Because every student in my classroom is reading her or her own book, I must converse with each of them in order to determine their progress toward reading goals and give them the individual support they need. I cannot wait for weeks to discover that Danny is not reading or that Kaitlin abandoned her last four books. If I waited for the products of our reading activities such as book reviews or independent strategy practice to discover that some of my students were struggling to read their books or understand them, it would be too late. Through conferences and reading response entries, I assess whether students are enjoying their books and comprehending them. This exchange between my students and me has a common jumping-off place: our reader's notebooks.

The reader's notebook we use, a customized version of Fountas and Pinnell's *Guiding Readers and Writers (Grades 3–6)*, is a seventy-page spiral notebook with photocopies of charts and lists trimmed and glued into the front. The notebook has several sections for recording students' reading activities:

- *Tally list:* This page is divided into columns for the genres and number of titles I require students to read. Students tally the books they have read as they go, and I sign off on any genre requirements that they complete.

- *Reading list:* This list is where students record all of the books they have read or attempted and abandoned. Each book's entry includes the title, author, date the book was finished, and the student's assessment of how difficult the book was to read.

- *Books-to-read list:* This list serves as a shopping list or plan for a student's future reading. Students record sequels that are yet to be published, books recommended by peers or me, or books that they have previewed and want to read later.

- *Response entries:* The majority of the reader's notebook is dedicated to response entries. The focus of these letters is aesthetic; students reflect on their personal reactions to the books they read and on the authors' writing. I write letters that respond back, asking questions and digging into students' interpretations and appreciation of their books.

I make a notebook for myself, too. I record all of the books I read from the beginning of summer to the end of one school year and carry the notebook with me to class every day. During book commercials (on-the-spot book recommendations by students), I list any books students recommend that I would like to read, and I access my notebook during conferences and class discussions when a student needs the name of an author or a recommendation about a book they know I have read. In the section of my notebook that corresponds to the one where students write their response entries, I write conference notes instead. Students grab their notebooks every day at the beginning of class and refer to them constantly, adding books, checking off reading requirements, or drafting responses. When we meet for conferences, I expect students to bring their notebook so we can look at it together and talk about it. And I bring mine.

MY CLASSROOM IS AN anthill—alive, bustling, each member working independently, yet united in our common purpose: reading. An undercurrent of students' voices, whispering to one another, reinforces the feeling of industry and meaningful work. Josh and Jon stretch out across a pile of beanbags in one corner, wrapped up in their books. Courtney and Lauren sit on the couch, heads together, reading *What My Mother Doesn't Know*, Sonya Sones's latest book of narrative poetry. Bishop sits at the computer, skimming Amazon for quotes he can cite in his book review of *Peak*. Jacob and Madison are updating their reading lists. Daniella is writing a response letter. The students' writing and conversations are a natural progression from the reading that they are doing. I sit in the center, perched on my green director's chair, chatting with Eric about his latest book, *Dr. Jekyll and Mr. Hyde*, and his experiences in reading such a challenging work:

"The vocabulary in *Dr. Jekyll and Mr. Hyde* is pretty complicated. How did you get through it?"

"Well, some of the words I looked up, and some I skipped; I could get the idea."

"Did you find yourself rereading parts of it?"

"Yeah. I read slower, too."

"Eric, those strategies you used—reading more slowly, looking up words, skipping words when you found clues to the meaning—those are all strategies that readers use when they come across words they don't know."

"It took me a while, but I was proud of myself for finishing it."

Eric and I talk about what he plans to read next—Michael Crichton's contemporary adult science fiction novels *Jurassic Park* and *The Lost World*—and I dash off a few comments in my notebook about his use of reading strategies to define unknown vocabulary.

Our conferences are born in students' notebooks, where they write response entries to me once a week and turn them in. (See Figure 4.2 for an example of a response entry.) I study each child's reading progress in greater detail by looking at the first three sections of their notebook.

These pages tell me about a student's reading momentum. I look for holes in reading lists and note trends that may indicate whether the student is finishing books or avoiding particular genres like biography or poetry. When I see that a student is having problems getting through books, sticking too closely to a genre, or not making plans for future reading, I consider whether the student is stalled.

After school, I dig through the milk crate under my desk, where students turn in their notebooks to me, and pull Molly's from the top of the pile. Her recent response letter makes me smile. Molly is reading Cornelia Funke's *Inkheart* because I suggested it to her. We have come a long way from the first weeks of school, when I plied her with book after book and she rejected them all. She was suspicious of any book I recommended back then. Now she knows my suggestions come from a reader's enthusiasm, not a teacher's agenda. Her entry (see Figure 4.2) provides valuable clues about Molly as a reader and what she takes away from the book she is reading.

molly #4　　　　　　　　　　　　5-12-08
miller

Dear Mrs. Miller,
　　　I am in the process of reading
Inkheart! I absolutley LOVE this book!!
I am at the part where Fengolio
& Meggie read the tin soldier back
into the re-written, happy ending, story.
They are now trying to figure out a
way to change Inkheart into making
the Shadow kill Capricorn. I am
eager to see how it ends! I
know there is a sequel called Inkspell.
Is that worth my time to read?
　　　I thought the Thief Lord
was a little slow in the beginning
but I liked the middle a lot! I
thought it was cool how at first
they were in the abandoned movie
theatre & then moved to the Lady's
house. I also liked how the detective
was so niced to the kids and was on
their side. I liked the way the author
wrote the part when Bo was taken by
their Aunt. It really showed the love connection
between Bo & Prosper!
　　　　　　　Sincerley,
　　　　　　　　Molly

FIGURE 4.2: *Extract from the Reader's Notebook of a Student.*
Source: Molly, grade 6.

I see that Molly can repeat the events of *Inkheart*, a basic comprehension skill, but her entry reveals much more. Her anticipation for the ending shows her engagement with the story and her investment in its outcome. By soliciting advice about whether she should read the sequel, Molly reveals our trusting reader-to-reader relationship.

I have fond memories of reading *Inkheart*, too, and I am pleased that Molly enjoys it as much as I had hoped. My curiosity about her personal connections with the book forms the basis for my response:

Dear Molly,

I enjoyed *Inkheart*, too! It is one of my favorite books (I know I say this all of the time, but I mean it!). I have never read a book which explores the power of reading to change your life (both negatively and positively) in such an interesting way. I always ask readers of *Inkheart* which book they would read themselves into if they could. Do you have a favorite story you would like to visit? Which character is your favorite? Can you guess who mine is? *Inkspell* is wonderful, and certainly worth reading, but you might want to take a break between *Inkheart* and the sequel. Both books are so long!

No inauthenticity here; obviously, I have read *Inkheart*. My conversational tone with Molly about a book we have both enjoyed and my advice about reading *Inkspell* reinforces our bond as readers. I ask Molly high-level comprehension questions that require her to evaluate and analyze the book and her impressions of it.

These letters are exchanges between a more experienced reader and a less experienced reader, not a list of questions probing whether or not Molly read the book. I challenge Molly to think more deeply about the book, but from the stance of a more advanced reader who read *Inkheart*, too. Readers whispering back and forth about their reading experiences—this is how reading should look.

CHAPTER 5

Walking the Walk

When I look back, I am so impressed again with the life-giving power of literature. If I were a young person today, trying to gain a sense of myself in the world, I would do that again by reading, just as I did when I was young.

—Maya Angelou

I feel really bad about all those good books out there waiting for me to read them.

—Parker

RETURNING FROM WINTER BREAK, my students gather around me in the hall. "Well, did you make it?" Madison asks me, referring to my goal of reading one book for each of the twelve days of the holiday.

"No, I didn't. I only read eight."

"Only eight? Only eight," Jon laughs at me, shaking his head.

"Yeah, I got bogged down in a book I wasn't enjoying, and I started to read less so that I wouldn't have to deal with it," I admit.

"What book was it, Mrs. Miller?" someone asks.

"*The True Meaning of Smekday*—it's on a lot of hot book lists for this year, and it's about alien invasion; you would have thought it would have been more exciting, but it just drags and drags."

Stacey pipes up, "That happened to me when I tried to read *Uglies*. I know that all of the girls rave about that book, but I just couldn't get into it."

Turning back to me, Madison asks, "So, what did you do?"

"I set it off to the side and read *The Higher Power of Lucky* instead! Hey, Riley, I finished *Marly's Ghost*, too; thanks for recommending it to me. I loved it, but it was sad!"

Riley laughs, "I know!"

"Does anyone else want to read *Smekday*?" I ask them. "I bet it would be good for another reader, but I am going to abandon it."

Several students clamor to get the book from me, and I pass it on. My students like to read the books that I read and recommend to them, but they also like to read the books that I have abandoned and prove me wrong. A few years back, Jared strutted around the entire year because he read and loved *The Last Book in the Universe*, by Rodman Philbrick, a speculation on a possible future without books. I had renamed this book *The Last Book I Will Ever Finish* because I had abandoned it twice. Jared declared it was one of his favorites and got several other students to read it, too.

The Need for Reading Role Models: The Crux of the Reading Crisis

My credibility with students and the reason they trust me when I recommend books to them stems from the fact that I read every day of my life and that I talk about reading constantly. I am not mandating an activity for them that I do not engage in myself. I do not promote reading to my students because it is good for them or because it is required for school success. I advocate reading because it is enjoyable and enriching. When my students think about me in the future, I want them to remember me as a reader with a book in my hand and a recommendation on my lips.

The relationships I build with my students are predominantly those of one reader to another. I am so enthusiastic about reading, so joyful about books, so willing to share my opinions and my reading experiences that my students are swept up in my love of books and want to feel it for themselves. We talk about books together all day, from the first moment I greet students in the hall until we pack up books to read at home each night. My students laugh at me when I stagger into class bleary-eyed and tell them that I stayed up too late reading my latest book. They may laugh, but they also see that reading is something I value enough to lose sleep over.

Findings from a 2007 Associated Press poll, reported in the *Washington Post*, indicate that the average adult American read only four books that entire year. This statistic does not tell the whole story; of the adults who read, their average was seven books, but

25 percent of the respondents did not read a book at all (Fram, 2007). Teachers fare no better on surveys of adult reading behaviors than the general population; in the 2004 article "The Peter Effect," Anthony and Mary Applegate report that of the preservice teachers whom they studied, 54.3 percent were unenthusiastic about reading, leaving little hope that these teachers would be able to inspire students to engage in an activity they themselves did not enjoy. This data is all the more alarming when you consider that "one of the key factors in motivating students to read is a teacher who values reading and is enthusiastic about sharing a love of reading with students" (Gambrell, 1996). What is going on here? Why aren't adults, even teachers, reading, and what is this doing to our students?

We have created a culture of reading poverty in which a vicious cycle of aliteracy has the potential to devolve into illiteracy for many students. By allowing students to pass through our classrooms without learning to love reading, we are creating adults (who then become parents and teachers) who don't read much. They may be capable of reading well enough to perform academic and informational reading, but they do not love to read and have few life reading habits to model for children.

Who will be our future role models for reading if we don't produce any from our classrooms? It is popular to blame parents for their children's disengagement from reading, but even parents who read to their children, take them to libraries, and model good reading habits at home have difficulty overcoming a reading wasteland in their children's classrooms, where teachers may not read. Under these circumstances, there is little opportunity for their children to develop lifelong reading habits at school. When I walk into my daughter's third-grade classroom on Meet the Teacher night and don't see a single book for students to read in sight, I know that this year role modeling for independent reading is going to come from me, not her new teacher. What about students who do not have parents who read? What about the parents who never learned to love reading themselves and have little to offer their own children in the way of being a role model for reading? Who takes responsibility for them?

Teachers bemoan students' lack of reading experiences before they enter school and students' lack of support for their reading at home. But teachers never seem to take ownership of the fact that the parents of these students, the very individuals we believe should be role models for reading, were once our students, too. When students walk into my classroom having never read a book or when their reading diet consists solely of *The Day My Butt Went Psycho* and Garfield cartoons, I know that there is an absence of knowledgeable, enthusiastic role models for reading in their lives—not just in their homes, but in their classrooms, too. Readers are made, not born. Few students spring out of the ground fully formed as readers. They need help, and we cannot assume that they will get it from home, but they should always get it from us, their teachers.

What Does Reading Mean to You?

There is evidence that a teacher's views on *what reading is* affect students' perceptions of reading and their long-term interest in it, too. Rosenblatt's transactional theory—which analyzes how readers approach a text and what purpose they have for reading it—defines two types of readers: efferent readers and aesthetic readers. Teachers who take an efferent stance see reading as a way to acquire knowledge, diving into a text for the purpose of getting information out of it. These teachers present reading as a series of skills to be mastered, processes to be fine-tuned and applied in order to collect information. There are a million and one books that show teachers this nuts-and-bolts approach to teaching reading. I see this skill-based approach as an outside-to-inside way of reading, a method of attacking each reading event with a to-do list of strategies in the hope that this will lead students to comprehension.

Teachers who take an aesthetic stance to reading—in other words, those who see reading as an emotional and intellectual journey—approach literacy instruction differently. This inside-to-outside look at reading considers each reader's personal impressions of what they read and their tastes and preferences. Both methodologies have benefits when working with young readers; after all, readers access texts for different purposes, both informational and experiential, in turn.

You needn't look any further than a classroom to see these alternating philosophies at work. Are the children capable of reading well enough for academic purposes? Do they spend much time pleasure reading in class? How many of the students choose to read outside of school? Do the teachers read? Most teachers who are not readers themselves take a skills-based approach. They may never talk to their students about loving books and craving reading, but tell them instead about the need to read well to get along in school and in life. But when you consider that the teachers who have an aesthetic view of reading have the greatest influence on their students' motivation and interest in reading (Ruddell, 1995) and have more impact on the long-term reading habits of their students than those who see reading as a skill to be mastered, the instructional edge goes to the teacher who sees reading as a gift, not a goal.

The Teacher Leads the Way

Motivation to read and attitudes toward reading are not the only areas in which teachers' reading habits and views on reading affect their students' reading behaviors. Lundberg and Linnakyla (1993, cited in Applegate and Applegate, 2004) found a link between the reading habits of teachers and the reading achievement of their students. When my principal interviews candidates for a teaching position at my school, regardless of whether it's a language arts position, he always asks them to discuss the last book they read. He recognizes the importance of putting role models for reading in front of students every day. While teaching preparation programs impart methodologies for reading pedagogy to teachers, my principal recognizes that our lives as readers are a powerful component in our ability to teach reading, too.

Students need lots of modeling and practice in how to read different types of texts, but showing them how to read is not the only act we must model for our students. If we want our students to read and enjoy it for the rest of their lives, then we must show them what a reading life looks like. If our reading experiences inform our views on what reading is, it is helpful to evaluate our reading attitudes and behaviors.

Finding Your Inner Reader

In taking a look at your self-reflection responses, what have you learned about yourself as a reader? Is reading just a tool to access information and be successful in school and work, or is it also a pleasurable escape for you? Consider how your view of reading seeps into your classroom and colors your instruction. Is your view of reading reflected in the literacy activities you use with students? If you see reading as a tool, try to incorporate opportunities for your students to read for pleasure, too.

If you have negative memories of reading in school as a child, how do these experiences show up in your teaching? You may not see the value of reading as a pleasurable endeavor because you were never inspired to read for enjoyment. It is also possible that your negative experiences as a young reader have steeled your resolve to do a better job of motivating your own students. It may be the reason you became a teacher! Share your reading struggles with your students, and describe how you overcame them.

If you have fond memories of reading as a child, how do you share these memories with your students? How has your early love of reading carried into your adult life? If it hasn't, why not? Take a look at why you no longer enjoy reading as much as you did or no longer carve out time to do it.

If you are still an enthusiastic reader, I imagine that you can point to some positive experiences with books as a child, even if these encounters did not occur at school. I can close my eyes and bring up Garth Williams's illustrations in my much-read copy of Laura Ingalls Wilder's *Little House in the Big Woods*. My sisters and I still laugh when remembering our attempts to live like pioneers in our backyard after reading the Little House books. When recommending *A Wrinkle in Time*, by Madeline L'Engle, to my students, I share with them that I did a book report on it in seventh grade, complete with a demonstration of a tesseract—using string to represent the folding of time and space, just like in the book. My lifelong obsession with fantasy and science fiction began with this book.

SELF-REFLECTION ACTIVITY

What were your reading experiences as a child?

Were these positive or negative experiences for you?

Do you see yourself as a reader now?

How do you share your reading experiences—both current experiences and those from the past—with your students?

With which group of readers in your classroom do you most identify—the underground readers, the developing readers, or the dormant readers?

Who have been your role models for reading?

List the last five books you have read.

How long did it take for you to read these books?

Which books were read for a job or for a school-related purpose?

Which books were read for pleasure?

I still list both books on my top ten favorites list, although I have read thousands of books since.

If you do love to read but never share this with your students, why not? Don't do what I did in those first few years and leave your inner reader at home because you are afraid that no one at your school will get what you are doing. We don't want our students to compartmentalize their reading lives—one for school and one for home—and we should not do it, either. Your love of reading is the best part of you. You can use your knowledge of reading and books to forge connections with students who are still forming a self-concept as readers and need a strong role model to follow. It is the most important resource you bring to class each day.

Reading Improvement Plan

Even if you have never been an avid reader or have lost your zeal for reading over the years, it is not too late to develop a love of reading. "Fake it until you make it," and take an academic stance if it helps. Craft your own reading plan. If you're having trouble getting started, here are some steps you can take:

- *Commit to a certain amount of reading per day:* When I am on the road at a conference or at a speaking engagement, I often hear teachers proclaim that they do not have time to read, but I believe that we can always find time for what we value. Set aside fifteen minutes per day while dinner is cooking or when you are on the treadmill. Can you get up fifteen minutes earlier or stay up fifteen minutes later? How about when you are waiting for your children at soccer or ballet practice? Do you have time during your commute? Why not read during your bus or train ride, as my husband does? I read at night after our daughters are in bed. Grab a few minutes in class each day, and read alongside your students.

- *Choose books to read that are personally interesting to you:* Resist the urge to choose a book because you think you can use it later for school. The same goes for reading books on pedagogy or a topic you may teach. This reading plan is about finding the joy in reading, not work. If you cannot find any books that interest you, talk to colleagues or friends who read more than you and ask them for recommendations. Check out displays in bookstores and libraries, too. Join a book club, or start one with your colleagues. Start reading book reviews.

- *Read more books for children:* If you loved to read as a child, revisit the types of books that you fell in love with in the first place. I like to read children's books because the stories and the characters are more innocent and pure than those I find in adult fiction. Plus, these books almost always end happily! If you did not learn to love to read as a child, you were cheated out of a joyful experience. Reclaim it. My friend Jen Robinson, author of the Web site "Jen Robinson's Book Page," has a powerful argument for why adults should read more children's books. According to Jen, adults who did not read as children have missed out on part of their cultural heritage, the opportunity for inspiration, and a means of communication with the young people in their lives. Even though she is not a classroom teacher, Jen's views reflect what life readers know.

   Naturally, if you read more children's books, you will suggest some of the books you have read to your students or read a great book that you have discovered with them. Students will be grateful that you are interested in the same books that they love, too. When I'm reading children's or young adult books, I think about which students in my classroom would like to read the book next. Nothing inspires my students to read more than when I hand one of them a book and say, "I just finished this, and I know that you will like it."

WHY YOU SHOULD READ CHILDREN'S BOOKS AS AN ADULT

BY JEN ROBINSON

1. It's fun.

2. It keeps your imagination active.

3. It strengthens your relationship with the children in your life who read.

4. It sets an example for the children in your life, making them more likely to become readers.

5. It clues you in on cultural references that you may have missed (both current and classical).

6. It's fast. Children's books are usually shorter than adult books, so if you don't think you have time to read, you DO have time to read children's books.

7. It allows you to read across genres. Children's books aren't limited to mystery OR science fiction OR fantasy OR literary fiction. They can have it all.

8. It's like time travel—it's an easy way to remember the child that you once were, when you first read a book.

9. It's often inspirational—reading about heroes and bravery and loyalty makes you want to be a better person. And couldn't we all do with some of that?

10. Did I mention that it's fun?

Source: Jen Robinson's Book Page, 2005.

- *Take recommendations from your students:* When choosing young adult or children's literature to read, ask your students what they would recommend to you. I have stacks of books that students have loaned me to read. They are always surprised when they have read a book that I haven't, and they are always eager to expand my book horizons with their titles. I currently have twelve books stacked on Miller Mountain that students have loaned me to read, and I assure you, they expect a full report when I am done!

You gain a lot of insight about the reading habits and preferences of your students—including what genres they enjoy, what series they are devoted to, the reading level of their books, and the quality of the reading material they read most—when you read what they are reading. You can also find many opportunities to expand students' reading horizons by looking at what they are not reading as well as what they are. By identifying the genres that students avoid reading or by analyzing whether the books that students choose to read are too easy or too hard, you can identify areas in which you can help students grow as readers.

- *Investigate recommendations from industry sources:* I have a love-hate relationship with book lists. Any book list is immediately dated, and it is hard to maintain a list of suggested titles that is not obsolete the moment it is published. For that reason, I am reluctant to publish any sort of recommended reading list for teachers who want an entry point; however, if you turn to Appendix B, you will see that my students have shared their "Ultimate Library List," which is full of marvelous recommendations. It is important to stay current on the books available for students to read—what is new and culturally relevant as well as tried-and-true classics. Scores of titles are mentioned in this book. You can draw from any of the resources I have mentioned to create a basic list of titles that have proven to be engaging for students.

I use Internet sites and book industry magazines as sources of recommendations because they are usually updated or published often. I find that the books of lists I use, like Blasingame's *Books That Don't Bore 'Em*, often contain descriptions that are useful for matching books to readers, interviews with notable authors, or other information that remains useful to me after the lists become outdated.

USEFUL BOOKS AND WEBSITES

- *Association for Library Services to Children: Literary Awards* (www.ala.org/ala/alsc/awardsscholarships/literaryawds/literaryrelated.cfm). This Web site is home to the Newbery, Caldecott, Printz, Coretta Scott King, and other book awards given by the American Library Association each year. The site includes extensive summaries and the complete list of the current and former award winners and honor medalists. The Newbery list alone is a gold mine of the best American literature of the past century for children.

- *Books That Don't Bore 'Em: Young Adult Books That Speak to This Generation* (Blasingame, 2007). With lists of books on topics like "Living Against the Grain" and "Misfits and Outcasts," Blasingame provides an overview of popular books that tap into the social issues and personal interests of young adults. More than just lists, this text includes in-depth interviews with popular authors such as Avi and Nancy Farmer, as well as tips on how to pick high-quality, high-interest books for your students and you.

- *Goodreads* (www.goodreads.com). Goodreads is a free social networking site for readers. Members create bookshelves of books they have read, are reading, or plan to read, and share lists with their invited friends. This endless repository of book reviews, contests, and lists feeds the most avid bibliophiles. I share books and lists with former students and teachers across the country and often browse the lists and bookshelves of my friends for new books.

- *Jen Robinson's Book Page* (http://jkrbooks.typepad.com/). Jen, who has a Ph.D. in industrial engineering and co-founded her own software company, is the life reader we all hope to raise. Her prolific blog and Web postings are filled with detailed reviews and personal reflections about the world of children's books, their authors, and children's book publishing. She reads more than I do, and her taste in books is spot on. I follow her blog closely just to find out what she is reading!

- *teenreads.com* (www.teenreads.com/). This Web site is not meant for teachers; it is meant for students. The futuristic layout and features like "Videos/Podcasts," "Cool & New," and the monthly poll skillfully integrate the latest networking tools to create a fun, modern site about reading for today's teen readers. Check out the up-to-date "Ultimate Teen Reading" list for over 250 books that were voted perfect reading choices by readers of the site. I use the "New in Paperback" and "Coming Soon" links to stay ahead of my students on the latest books.

- *Create your own reader's notebook:* At the start of each year, when my students are trimming and gluing their own reader's notebooks, I make a new one for myself. I record all of the books I have read or abandoned for an entire year in one notebook, just like I ask my students to do. Each notebook serves as a record of what I have read over the years, and I use my reading lists to order books for the class library or make recommendations to my students and friends.

- *Reflect on what you are reading:* I am not suggesting that you write summaries of every book you read or your personal responses to them, but you can, if you would like to. Think about what you are reading, and observe what you like about the book or what you don't like about it. What makes it challenging or fun to read? What sticks with you about the book when you are done?

Share Your Struggles

In addition to the tips I mentioned in the preceding section, I find it important to share my reading challenges with my students. When I read *The Time Traveler's Wife* with my book club, I talked with my students about how challenging the book was for me to read. I enjoyed it tremendously, but the shifts between narrators and the setting changes made it hard for me to follow. I revealed how I had to slow down my reading pace and focus on the details more than I would have with a chronological narrative. They were surprised to learn that I, too, experience difficulties when reading.

Share with your students what you enjoy about the books you read, what makes them hard for you, and what strategies you use to get through challenging reading material. Students feel inadequate when they have to struggle. Knowing about your reading challenges can help boost their self-esteem. I have seen teachers "fake model" the experience of having reading obstacles with their students while guiding them through test practices. Students know that a teacher does not struggle through a fifth-grade-level reading passage, and faking it only serves to lessen their trust. It's better to be honest.

Standing off to the side and telling students to read doesn't work for most of them. How are they supposed to become readers if they don't have any models to emulate? Remember that you are the best reader in the room, the master reader. Embrace that, and wear your reading love proudly in front of your students every day. The reality is that you cannot inspire others to do what you are not inspired to do yourself.

CHAPTER 6

Cutting the Teacher Strings

Reading is not a duty, and has consequently no business to be made disagreeable.

—Augustine Birrell

I think my worst nightmare was last year, when we all had to read the same book, and do worksheets, and make journals after every chapter.

—Christina

IN THE FALL OF 2007, the National Institutes of Health awarded $30 million to four research centers—the University of Colorado at Boulder, Florida State University, the University of Houston, and Baltimore's Kennedy Krieger Institute—in an attempt to uncover why reading interest declines and ability dips as students approach adolescence (Samuels, 2007). While I cannot fully explain this demotivation or why it happens to so many children, I can tell you who to ask about it: the children themselves.

Over the course of my teaching career, students have told me consistently that reading as it is traditionally taught and assessed actually encourages them to hate reading. My student Skylar told me during a conference, "What makes reading painful is when it takes longer to do reading worksheets about a book than to actually *read* a book." And Dana shared her previous experiences in fifth grade: "Every day we would read a chapter of a book and spend the rest of the day either discussing [it] or doing worksheets. When book reports came around, I read the book in two days and finished the book report by the end of the week. We still had to work on it two weeks later, and I had nothing to do."

Reading has become schoolwork, not an activity in which students willingly engage outside of school. Teachers tie so many strings to reading that students never develop a pleasurable relationship to reading inside or, regrettably, beyond the classroom. Referring to the endless activities piled onto reading books in school, my student Jordan writes, "I want to scream, this doesn't help us!"

Seeing the Wallpaper

My principal often asks us, his teaching staff, to examine traditional practices and question whether these practices are what educational policy leader Richard Elmore calls "unexamined wallpaper"—classroom practices and institutional policies that are so entrenched in school culture or a teacher's paradigm that their ability to affect student learning is never probed. Are the activities and assessments we use accomplishing our intended instructional goals, or are they simply what we have always done?

As I mentioned in Chapter Three, whenever I encounter a practice that is widespread in reading classes, I consider what the goal of the practice is and then look at ways to reposition the practice so that it is more motivating to my students and more in line with my personal beliefs about reading and the habits and skills shown by life readers, not just school readers.

Let's unpack some of the tried-and-true (they have definitely been tried, but are they really true?) language arts standbys and examine their intended learning goals. In addition, let's consider alternatives that accomplish the same goals but are more in keeping with the habits of true readers and what matters most to students.

Traditional Practice: Whole-Class Novels

We shouldn't teach great books; we should teach a love of reading.
—B. F. Skinner

Teachers build elaborate units of instruction around novels, breaking down a text into discrete concepts for closer study. If you are a new teacher, you might feel that your best hope for survival is that some wiser teacher will share these Rosetta Stones that decipher how you are supposed to teach reading, complete with all of the activities you need to "get students through" books. If you do not have a mentor teacher to feed you lesson plans, you need look no further than your local teacher supply store, where a wall of prepackaged novel units awaits you.

Some schools and school districts create lists of required novels for each grade level. These lists are revered as sacred law despite the fact that you cannot find a single national standard that requires students to read specific texts.

Teaching whole-class novels does not create a society of literate people. Take a poll of your friends and relatives (those who did not become teachers), and ask them how they feel about the books they read in high school. Now, ask them how much they still read. In the *Phi Delta Kappan* article "Farewell to *A Farewell to Arms*: Deemphasizing the Whole-Class Novel," Douglas Fisher and Gay Ivey question the widespread use of whole-class novels in reading classes, claiming, "Students are not reading more or better as a result of the whole-class novel. Instead, students are reading less and are less motivated, less engaged, and less likely to read in the future."

If reading a book together as a class doesn't improve students' reading ability or enjoyment of reading, what is the purpose of this practice? Some teachers assert that it is critical to expose students to great literature (think John Steinbeck, Mark Twain, Nathaniel Hawthorne) as part of their cultural heritage. How else can we motivate teenagers to read these authors on their own?

I don't disagree with this goal, in theory; after all, I had to smile when my teenage daughter, after reading *The Crucible*, referred to Salem in a joke. But is the ability to generate a pithy literary reference all she got from reading Arthur Miller's play? Reading historically and culturally significant literature enhances readers' background knowledge, to be sure, but at what cost? My teenager only reads the books she prefers in the summer because she is burdened with required reading during the school year. Consuming a literary diet built exclusively on the classics does not provide students with the opportunity to investigate their own personal tastes in reading material and narrows their perspective of reading to the school task of hyper-analyzing literature. There needs to be a balance between the need to teach students about literature and the need to facilitate their growth as life readers. What about the greater goal of encouraging students to read when the time for dissecting classics ends?

One Size Does Not Fit All

Indoctrination into the classic literary canon supersedes all other aims for the readers in our classrooms, it seems. Teachers can always point to a few students who love these classics, but I argue that they are a minority or that few *become future readers* as a result. Why would they? Every student that moves through our classes is not destined to become an English literature major, and we cannot gear our teaching as if they were. Using whole-class novel units as the primary method of delivering reading instruction has inherent problems. Witnessing these problems in my own class and others, and listening to the complaints my students have shared about whole-class novel units has led me to these truths:

- *No one piece of text can meet the needs of all readers.* A typical heterogeneous classroom may have a range of readers that spans four or more grade levels. It is impossible to find a book that is at an appropriate instructional level for all of these students. The only way to differentiate among such a diverse group of readers is through a more liberal selection of reading material.

- *Reading a whole-class novel takes too long.* A month or more of instruction around one text takes a lot of time that students could spend reading more books on a wider range of topics. The slowest reader in my sixth-grade classes needs only a week or so to complete a book at their reading level. You do the math.

- *Laboring over a novel reduces comprehension.* Breaking books into chapter-sized bites makes it harder for students to fall into a story. Few readers outside of school engage in such a piecemeal manner of reading.

- *Not enough time is spent reading.* Many novel units are stuffed with what Lucy Calkins calls "literature-based arts and crafts," extensions and fun activities that are meant to engage students but suck up time in which students could be reading or writing.

- *Whole-class novels ignore students' interest in what they like to read.* Reading becomes an exercise in what the teacher expects you to get out of the book they chose for you, a surefire way to kill internal motivation to read.

- *Whole-class novels devalue prior reading experience.* What about the students who have already read the book? Admittedly, this may be a small number of readers, but I have sixth graders who have already read *To Kill a Mockingbird* and *The Outsiders*—two books that I know are taught in upper grades. Are they going to be expected to read them again? Advanced readers deserve the opportunity to continue their growth as readers, too.

Yes, students benefit from the deep analysis of literature that a thorough look at one book provides, but there needs to be a balance between picking a book apart to examine its insides and experiencing the totality of what a book offers. There are other paths to teaching critical analysis and reading skills than belaboring one book for weeks. Let's not lose sight of our greater goal: inspiring students to read over the long haul.

Alternative: Rethinking the Whole-Class Novel

My first suggestion on the topic of whole-class novels would be to evaluate whether you are truly required to read certain texts with your students or whether this is just a tradition. When your department has invested budget money and time in a closetful of whole-class novel sets, it is hard to break away from the entrenched attitude that reading the same book across the grade level is the best instruction for students.

If your school district, language arts department, or school culture requires you to read certain texts with your students, look for ways to provide support to students who may not be able to read the book on their own, and limit the amount of time spent reading the book.

Some ways to compromise:

- *Read the book aloud to students.* Your ability to fluently read a text that is inaccessible or challenging to many students aids their comprehension, vocabulary development, and enjoyment. Students can apply their mental effort to building meaning from the book instead of decoding the language.

- *Share-read the book.* Share-reading involves you reading aloud to students while they each follow along in their own copy. In addition to providing the benefits of read-alouds, share-reading may increase students' reading speed because they have to keep up with a reader who reads at a faster rate than they do. In addition, students' sight recognition of vocabulary improves because unknown words are pronounced for them. Again, students' focus can be steered toward comprehension rather than decoding.

- *Take a critical look at arts and crafts activities and extension projects.* Any activity that does not involve reading, writing, or discussion may be an extra that takes away from students' development as readers, writers, and thinkers. In *What Really Matters for Struggling Readers*, Richard Allington reminds us, "When we plan to spend six weeks teaching *Island of the Blue Dolphins*, we plan to limit children's reading and fill class time with other activities."

- *Limit the number of literary elements and reading skills you explicitly teach with any one book* (Fisher and Ivey, 2007). Do not try to use one text to teach students everything they need to know about symbolism, characterization, or figurative language. Focus instruction on the elements and skills that students need to comprehend that specific text. The same goes for explicitly teaching scores of vocabulary words. I would rather expose my students to fifteen different texts to meet my instructional goals than beat one book into the ground, expecting it to demonstrate a multitude of literary concepts.

I cannot deny that there are merits to reading one book with an entire class of students: the text serves as an example for the skills and knowledge you are teaching; you create a common literacy experience to which you can make future connections; and reading a book together fosters community among your students and you. The balancing act involves looking for methods that honor these goals while removing the factors that make the whole-class novel a detrimental practice for students.

Alternative: Teaching Readers, Not Books

Our district allows teachers the freedom to choose the materials that we use to meet the instructional requirements of Texas's standards and the district's scope and sequence curriculum. Students must walk out of my class knowing how to read critically and write well, but how I choose to deliver that instruction is left to me. If, like me, you are only expected to teach standards, not specific books, consider these avenues:

- *Select one theme or concept that students are expected to understand, gather a wide range of texts on this topic, and form book groups.* I use book groups in language arts or social studies because this format allows me to teach the desired concept or skill and offer students different texts to reach those goals. Naturally, using universal themes or literary elements as the anchor for instruction instead of one text acknowledges the wide range of reading levels and interests in a classroom. I have found that this is the simplest way for a reading teacher to differentiate reading instruction.

   The first step in implementing book groups is to decide which concept or theme you need to teach. Write a few guiding questions that you want students to be able to answer as evidence that they have grasped the targeted concept from reading their book. Next, select books that are linked conceptually or thematically. Students will form groups based on their choices from the books you have gathered.

   To help students preview books, I use the book pass, an activity designed by Janet Allen. Students begin by selecting a book to preview, recording the title and author in a book pass log. Students preview the book, look at the blurb, read the first page or so, and flip through the book to look at the visuals. After the preview, students record a few notes about the book in their log and assign the book a star rating to indicate their interest in reading it.

   When I call time, students pass the book they were previewing to the student next to them and continue the preview process with the next book. After most of the books have been passed, students write the top three books they would like to read on the back of their book pass log and turn them in to me. I look over their choices to determine the study groups. I consider the reading levels of the selected books, and with the knowledge I have of the books and the capabilities of each student, I decide which book is the best fit. I also look at management issues such as the dynamics of each group and the number of copies I have of each title.

For example, while my class was studying World War II in social studies, I wanted my students to understand the range of perspectives on this conflict by reading a variety of books. Using the book pass, students selected books on World War II from our vast library and read them over eight days of reading workshop time in class. Each group set reading goals for its members through daily meetings, and if students needed to take their book home to keep up with their group, they did.

All writing and discussion among book group members, as well as the whole class, circled back to our two focus questions: "How were the characters (or people, if the book was nonfiction) in your book involved in the war?" and "What were the short-term and long-term consequences for them?" This issue-based study provided my students with the opportunity to evaluate the points of view from books read by other students in addition to their own. We examined the perspectives of Japanese Americans, German soldiers, Holocaust victims, and children whose brothers and fathers fought in the war. I found that our classroom discussions about World War II were richer than if we had all read the same book because students came to the topic from different, often opposing viewpoints. My students walked away from the unit with a broader understanding of the war and its impact on all of the people touched by it.

- *Use short stories, excerpts, or poems to teach literary elements or reading skills, and ask students to apply their understanding to their independent books*. Using an instructional sequence of modeling, shared practice, and independent practice, what I model and practice with students always ends with application of a skill or evaluation of a concept, using their self-selected books.

When teaching the concept of literary conflict to my sixth graders, I cover the definitions of the types of conflict, drawing on examples from books and movies that are well known to them. Then, we read several short stories from our literature textbook, identify the conflicts in these stories, and analyze the resolutions in each. Students are then asked to go back to their independent novels, identify the story conflict (or conflicts), and evaluate how these conflicts were resolved. This process mirrors how teachers often use whole-class novels to teach literary concepts, with two marked differences: the modeling event took significantly less time than reading an entire book would, and the end point of my instruction led to independent reading, not ferreting out the same answers from the same book. Students who can demonstrate skill in this way show me not only that they understand the concepts of literary conflict and resolution but also that they comprehend the story they read—no book report needed.

I have learned that teaching a whole-class novel is not the best way to share literacy in a classroom because it disenfranchises students who cannot read the assigned book on their own or who have no interest in the book. Students passing books back and forth because they like them and find them to be meaningful, students begging you to read aloud to them, students arguing about the motives of the characters in their own books—all of these activities indicate that students are reading and getting everything out of reading that we wish for them to. My daily interactions with students tell me what I need to know.

Every concept and skill I teach, even when it involves grammar, connects back to students' independent work at some point, and I feel that this independent work must be self-selected reading and writing events, not the shorter goal of a worksheet or test practice. If not, how will I ever know to what extent they have grasped my instruction? It follows that this style of teaching fosters my students' independence and frees me from designing assessments and activities for all of the readers in my classroom. I could never design assessments for sixty students that demonstrate what students know as well as their application of reading strategies and literary concepts to their own books does. If you cannot find a method for assessing students that uses authentic texts, I would ask why that concept is worth teaching.

Traditional Practice: Comprehension Tests

For countless students, successful scores on a comprehension test are the culminating goal of every book they have ever read in school. Instead of savoring the books they've read or celebrating what they've learned from them, the ability to pass these tests becomes students' purpose for reading. Comprehension tests feed into a classroom cycle of assign it, then assess it. But where is the learning and teaching in that cycle? Teachers assign these summative assessments in order to motivate students to read and to determine whether students did, in fact, read a book. Where is the joy that we hope reading will engender in students?

We cannot confuse assessment techniques with motivation techniques, either. Reading for the goal of performing is not motivating for students beyond their desire to earn a good grade on the test and may actually reduce their reading enjoyment and enthusiasm for reading outside of school. After all, how many adult readers would choose to read if they had to take a multiple-choice test for every book they finished? Imagine how the alarming amount of television that Americans watch would decline if completion of a test were required after each program!

Retention of details about the characters or plot of a book may be part of the comprehension process, but regurgitating facts does not show that the reader has grasped the nuances of the themes in a book or gotten anything meaningful (or pleasurable) out of reading it. I have many former students who were involved in computer-based reading incentive and testing programs once they reached middle school. They tell me of their hatred for the programs and how they cheat (successfully, I might add) on the tests by sharing the answers with each other, without ever having read the book.

Programs like Accelerated Reader or Scholastic Reading performance counts, in which books are assigned a point value and students must complete a multiple-choice test after reading them, are the worst distortion of reading I can think of. Although proponents of these programs claim that students have reading freedom, the truth is that a student's selection of a book is limited by its point value and whether a test exists for it. Hence, developing students struggle to collect enough points to meet the teacher's requirements, and underground readers are bound to the books for which an Accelerated Reader test exists. These programs, which are reading-instruction wallpaper in many schools, send a message to young readers that a book's value lies in how many points it is worth, and reduce comprehension to a series of low-level trivia bites gleaned from the book. How does this sort of program prepare students for reading in the world outside of school?

Furthermore, shifting the purpose for reading a book toward the memorization of plot details and away from an overall appreciation for the book changes how students read. Instead of falling into a book and traveling on a journey with the characters, readers float on the surface of the story and cherry-pick moments they predict they will be tested on later.

Short of reading mountains of books and writing tests yourself, how can you determine whether students have read a book and comprehended it? As I described earlier in this chapter, I ask students to show their understanding of the literary elements that I have taught them in class by delving into their own books. Students cannot do this effectively if they have not read and comprehended the book.

A Word About Practice for Standardized Tests

We live in a world of standardized testing. My students will eventually be expected to show the concepts and strategies that they have learned during my class on the Texas Assessment of Knowledge and Skills at the end of the year. I do not worry about this end goal much because I know that the amount of reading and response that my students do is the best preparation for this assessment. Frankly, the state's goal is narrower than mine. The state assessment measures only a small number of the standards that the state prescribes that I teach. I want students to become life readers, people who read avidly.

I know that students who read widely and can talk and think critically about the books they are reading have little trouble doing well on standardized reading assessments, and my students reinforce my beliefs by acing the state test every year. I am not just talking about the gifted readers, either; I am talking about students who had failed the test the year before and were at risk of failing it again. I have no issue with standardized testing per se; I believe that students who cannot pass the minimal expectations set by these tests are not good readers. What I have grown to mistrust is how the high-stakes nature of these tests has disrupted quality reading instruction.

In many classrooms, I see a shift from deep reading instruction with a wide range of materials to endless drilling and rote memorization of test-taking tricks. This is not teaching reading, it is teaching test taking. Many of these tricks are not transferable to any reading situation other than test reading and, therefore, do not prepare students for most of the reading that they must do beyond the test.

By sixth grade, most of my students have spent at least three years in classes in which test preparation and the drilling of test-taking strategies were the most common type of reading instruction they received. They have not read many books other than a few class novels. The opportunity for them to self-select reading material has been largely nonexistent. They have done almost no writing. Any activity that substantially replaces extensive reading, writing, and discourse in the classroom needs to be better than the activity that it replaces, and nothing, not even test prep, is better for students' reading ability than just plain reading, day after day. Endless test prep is the number one reason that students come to my class hating to read. They don't think test prep is one kind of reading; they think it is reading.

Test Reading as a Genre

Instead of narrowing my instructional focus to test prep, I prefer to teach reading standardized tests as its own genre. Here's how you read a map; here's how you read a newspaper article; and here's how you read a test. I spend a few weeks prior to the yearly standardized test on showing students how the tests are designed, discussing the different types of test questions, and examining the terms that are used in question stems. We talk about the skills and knowledge these tests are trying to assess and how to go about looking for the answers. I teach students how to read a test, but I do not teach reading through the test. Students should already have a foundation in all of the topics that will be assessed on a standardized test before they look at it. I don't think students should encounter literary terms for the first time in the context of a test question. When we talk about testing, we talk about how the test is designed to ask them about what they already understand about reading and literary analysis.

There are many ways to assess what students have learned, using measures that are tied to independent reading, although any assessment will have an air of artificiality to it; after all, life readers do not take assessments. The methods I suggest leave a smaller, less invasive footprint on the reader than the typical comprehension tests and book reports. The goals of all assessments should be to celebrate the accomplishments of readers, promote and plan for future reading, and foster the collaboration of a reading community.

Traditional Practice: Book Reports

In my opinion, the entire goal of a book report is for students to prove to the teacher that they actually read a book by demonstrating their ability to recite, in detail, all of the events or important facts from it. If a student is not a reader, how the book report motivates that student to pick up a book in the first place is never addressed. Some students do not read for many weeks and then power through a book in the days leading up to the due date for the report. They will hammer out a report, breathe a sigh of relief, and revert to a non-reading state until shortly before the next report is due. The report becomes an external motivator in which a grade creates pressure to read. In no way does that kind of motivation mirror the internal drive felt by life readers, for whom the pleasure of reading increases the desire to read. Reading lacks personal significance for students who see the report as the reason for reading—all stick and no carrot. Not only do the requirements for writing book reports fail to encourage students to develop consistent reading behaviors, but the reports are a chore to write and painful for the other students to listen to. After all, who wants to hear a complete summary of a book you may or may not have read? Book reports are also a bore to grade.

The Slippery Slope of Book Talks

Perhaps the tedium of book reports is why book talks have replaced book reports in many classrooms. The purpose of a book talk is not to prove to the teacher that you have read a book but to share with other readers a book you have read and persuade them to read it themselves. Recommending a book for the purpose of getting a friend to read it is more in alignment with what adult readers do when they finish a book.

Recognizing the inherent flaws in asking my students to do book reports, I implemented book talks for a time. However, I was still not happy with the results. Students, having already written and presented years of book report summaries, gave away too much information. At the other extreme, when students were asked to share their favorite moment from the book, I often heard, "My favorite part of the book was at the end."

Book talks did encourage some students to read the books their peers recommended, but I had to set aside at least two days of instructional time so that we could get through all the talks. Again, this was time when my students were not reading and writing. Invariably, several students had the same book to share, and we all had to sit through repeats. I taught my students the term *spoiler*, encouraging them not to give away so much information that no one would want to read the book after they finished talking about it. I then began to question whether the book talks were any better than the reports. I came to the conclusion that they were not. This realization coincided with the discovery that I could not duplicate the classroom design of experts in every respect. I needed to respond to my own observations and instincts about what did and did not work in my classroom.

Providing friends with enough information to interest them in reading a book and getting recommendations from other trusted readers are valid reasons for sharing opinions about books. When we distort this natural conversation among readers into one child standing at the front while all of the others sit up straight, stay quiet, and listen dutifully to hours of presentations, that free-flowing dialogue is lost. This is why I ditched both book reports and formal book talks and moved to book commercials and book reviews.

Alternative: Book Commercials

Book commercials are advertisements—short, impromptu testimonials from students about the books that they have read and enjoyed. (Think about how you might tell a friend about a book over lunch.) The intent of a book commercial is to provide students with a forum for sharing the books they love and for recommending those books to other readers in the class.

Once a week or so, often on Fridays at the end of class time, I will ask students whether anyone has a book to recommend to the class. As a means of sharing the books I have read that students might like to borrow, I often present my own book commercials for them. We talk about what I do not reveal about the book in these conversations, as well as what I do say. We also read lots of blurbs and teasers from the backs of books and jacket flaps in order to model our own conversations after these published examples.

Students can stand next to their desk or sit in my green director's chair (a rare treat) and informally share with the class about their book. If anyone else has read the same book, I ask that student to add their opinions of it, too. Students record any books from the commercials that interest them on the "Books to Read" pages of their reader's notebooks, and I do, too.

I keep a class roster on a clipboard and check off the students who share, making sure that everyone provides at least one commercial over the course of the grading period and that no individuals dominate the weekly discussions. I give everyone a grade for their book commercial; we all get to hear about books other readers like; and the entire experience lasts no more than twenty minutes a week. The students are excited to share their books, and we can all talk back and forth about them instead of listening passively to book talks or reports. I do not need to question the comprehension of students who give recommendations because their enthusiasm and strongly held opinions show me that they have read the book and responded to it authentically. If they disliked a book, they can share that, too!

Alternative: Book Reviews

I adore book reviews, as evidenced by the hours I spend each month poring over *Booklist* magazine and studying recommendations from Amazon and Goodreads on the Web. Consider book reviews authentic forums for celebrating books and sharing information about titles in your classroom, too. My students write book reviews and post them on their classroom blog, or they print newspaper column-sized versions and glue them inside the book itself, right alongside the blurbs and reviews of the professionals. While I might choose a book because *Publishers Weekly* has starred it, my students are more likely to pick a book that Riley or Eric recommended!

For the past week or so, my students have been reading professional book reviews and book jacket blurbs and teasers for the purpose of determining what information professionals include when evaluating books. We've made a chart of the criteria found in these reviews.

Jacob remarks that every book review he read included the word "compelling," so we add to our chart a list of words that reviewers include to entice the reader and make their

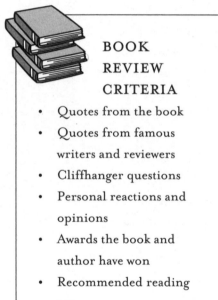

BOOK REVIEW CRITERIA

- Quotes from the book
- Quotes from famous writers and reviewers
- Cliffhanger questions
- Personal reactions and opinions
- Awards the book and author have won
- Recommended reading age
- Other books by the same author
- Comparisons with other books

book sound interesting: *compelling, action-packed, thrilling, thrill ride, exciting,* and *riveting.*

With a list of criteria from which to begin, students spend the next week composing their own book reviews (see Figures 6.1 and 6.2 for examples). I am asked to provide quotes for endless reviews because students know that I have read many of their books. I am careful to avoid using *compelling* to describe any book, though!

In order to inspire students to read when school requirements to do so are lifted, we must provide them with authentic opportunities to share with other readers what they love about the books they read. If our classroom practices only serve to assess whether or not students read—or to push our own instructional agenda—then we are doing little to encourage students to read. Traditional reading instruction that focuses on mandates outside of students and stirs fear-based motivation hijacks reading away from readers. Give it back to them.

Traditional Practice: Reading Logs

Many permutations of the reading log are used in classrooms, but all have common features. Students are asked to record how many minutes or pages they read over a given time period. Teachers require their students to read a certain number of minutes or pages per day, week, or grading period. Keeping these logs—whose purpose is for students to document their independent reading as proof to their teachers that they are reading—is an ineffective practice because recorded time spent reading is no proof that students actually read much. Students may write down how much or how long they read nightly but not finish many books. A conversation with my students during my first year of teaching revealed the futility of the home reading log. Simply put, the logs do not accomplish what they are supposed to accomplish. This

When I starting reading *Click Here* by Denise Vega, I couldn't stop! For the next 5 days, I read it any chance I could. *Click Here* is a very good suspenseful, page turner! *Click Here* is about a girl named Erin who is moving on to 7th grade this year. At her middle school, they separate the students' schedules by "tracks," track A, B or C. When she and her best friend Jilly get put on separate tracks, Erin thinks she is going to die! To make it worse, Jilly is sick on the first day of school so Erin has to go by herself. When Erin goes into her first class, she notices that there is a really cute guy in her class. So, now Erin is kind of glad Jilly is on a different track because now she won't always have to "compete" with Jilly to get guys to like her. Erin starts writing this online diary, but only she can see it, until it gets published on Molly Brown Middle School's website for EVERYONE to see. Read *Click Here* to find out the secrets of 7th grade. *Click Here* is a great book written for girls probably around the age of 12 to 14. I think every girl will like this book. In *Click Here* it talks about things that really happen in 7th grade. I got "addicted" to *Click Here* as soon as I started it. It was so good I want to read it again.

"Great Book. Funny Blog"—Jordan

FIGURE 6.1: *Riley's Review of* Click Here
Source: Riley, grade 6.

Inkspell is a captivating fantasy by Cornelia Funke. *Inkspell* is about a thirteen year old girl named Meggie, whose love for books and magical ability to bring the subject of any book to life, draw her to the Inkworld, a place of amazing sites and fantastic creatures where danger lurks around every corner. In the Inkworld, Meggie finds herself running from the menacing Basta, who is trying to get revenge on her for killing his former master, Capricorn. All fantasy lovers will simply adore this book. If you liked *Inkheart* or *Dragon Rider* (some of Cornelia's other masterpieces) then you will absolutely love *Inkspell*.

Michelle says: *Inkspell* is a compelling page turner. I couldn't put it down. It was one of my favorite books ever.

FIGURE 6.2: *Kenan's Review of* Inkspell
Source: Kenan, grade 6.

lesson was one of the first my students taught me. It went something like this:

"OK, guys, it's Friday—time to turn in your reading logs." Groans and the rifling of twenty-five papers ensue.

"Hey, Mrs. Miller, my dad forgot to sign my reading log."

"Well, I guess you will have to get him to sign it over the weekend and bring it back in on Monday.

I continue, "Doesn't your dad sign it every night? You are supposed to get it signed every night after you read."

"My dad says he doesn't have time to do that. I just have him sign it on Friday mornings when we are in the car." A classroom full of heads nodding in agreement tells me that this is a common practice.

"Are you telling me that your parents don't know whether you are reading every night or not? They are not keeping track of how much reading you are doing at home?"

"My mom believes me when I tell her I am reading. She just signs the log because you make us do it for a grade."

A chorus of "Yeah, me, too" circles the room.

Julie pipes up: "Mrs. Miller, I hate that log. I always forget to write down what I read each night, so I just sit down and fill it out the day we have to turn it in. I am not going to keep that log in bed with me at night so that I can write down what I read."

"Just because we fill out the log doesn't mean we actually did the reading," Amanda says.

When I questioned the rest of my students, it became clear that most of them were not keeping track of their daily reading in the log, and that most of their parents were not monitoring how much reading, if any, their children were doing at home. Lacking parent buy-in and perceived as a burden by students, the reading log begs to be fabricated. Deceitful, I suppose, but I imagine there are students in classrooms everywhere who fake their reading log at some point, even among those who read diligently. As a parent, I'll admit to signing papers hastily shoved into my hand by my daughters when we are in a mad rush to get out the door in the mornings.

Sadly, requiring parents to sign reading logs has failure written all over it. What I was really doing was assigning family homework, which is a hit-or-miss effort at best. As a new teacher, I assigned reading logs because it was what every other teacher did. How else would I monitor how much reading my students were doing?

The log is a reward for students who have strong home support for reading, but a punishment for those who don't. Thus, it never serves the students it's supposed to. Furthermore, in the case of my students who read at home each night but thought the log was a pain to maintain, it was a sign that I did not trust that they were reading when they said they were. No one wins in this battle.

So why assign logs in the first place? How did the reading log become such a ubiquitous practice? I see two reasons. Teachers require their students to keep reading logs because they think that parents will respond to the home reading requirement and monitor their children's reading more closely. Other teachers believe that mandating that students maintain and submit a reading log will motivate them to read.

Think long and hard about your students. I bet that the ones who are not keeping the log are those who you believe are not motivated readers, so this carrot-and-stick approach—require the accountability of the log, and they will read because of it—doesn't work. As long as the motivation to read sits outside the child, it will never be internalized. Don't be surprised if children who you know are capable, even avid readers, struggle with the log, too. These students prefer to spend their time reading, not accounting for their time. After a student spends an hour engrossed in a book, the log is a reminder that reading is a school job.

Why, then, are reading logs so popular among teachers? Because in theory, they provide us with tangible evidence that our students are engaged in independent reading. Yet they don't produce the outcome we are hoping for. The reality is that you can never mandate or monitor how much reading your students are doing at home. Yes, there will always be students and their parents who maintain the log because you require it, but there will also always be those for whom the log will serve only to discourage reading. Because it is an external motivation, the log never motivates students to read after the requirement is lifted. The bottom line: this log is about you, not your students. Logs don't give an accurate accounting of how much students are reading, and maintaining them does not motivate them to read more, either.

Alternative: Expanding Reading in Class

I expect my students to read at home for at least twenty minutes per night, but I never check on this or quiz them on whether they are doing it. I cannot effectively monitor this in any reasonable way. If a student is not making progress on his or her reading requirements or seems to spend an inordinate amount of time reading one book, I hold a conference with that student and ask about how much time he or she spends reading at home, but that is all.

As I discussed in Chapter Three, the only way to make sure that your students are reading every day is to set aside time for it in class. The only way you will know that your students read every day is to watch them read right in front of you. Daily reading is what transforms reading into a lifelong habit and builds reading ability—far preferable to bursts of reading as the sun sets on the night before a reading log is due. My students are more likely to continue reading a book at home when they have been reading it in school, too. I know this because they come to school excited about what they read the night before or groan that they stayed up too late reading again. Enthusiastic readers who eagerly tell me about what they read the night before are the only evidence I need that students are reading at home. The end-of-year evaluations I solicited from my students this year revealed that most of them were reading at home, even when I did not hold them accountable for it. Kenan declared, "I've read more books because of the time I get in class to read. I even read more at home because of it. I get to a really suspenseful part or toward the end [of the book] then I have to read it at home." They read because they want to, not because I make them.

Alternative: Freedom Within the Structure of a Reading Requirement

Setting some sort of goal for students' independent reading is a valid practice if the goal requires them to finish reading books. I have had students who would read and write every day in my class or record nightly reading in a log forever, and never actually complete a book or a piece of writing. Students are accomplished readers when they are able to express their feelings about the books they have read, not point to the number of hours they have spent doing time with a book. How does this work with a student who is struggling to meet his reading requirements? The following conversation with Jon illustrates how to encourage a student who is still not on board.

"I have only read six books this year," Jon complains, so that everyone in the room hears. "We are halfway through the year. I am never going to read forty books."

I could walk over to Jon and give him the reading pep talk, but I know there are others in class who could benefit from what I have to say, so I call back, "Jon, how many books did you read last year?"

"Hmm, two or three?"

Knowing that Jon is a sports fanatic, I ask, "Jon, if an athlete improved his performance 200 percent over one season, what would his coach say?"

"I guess he would think that was pretty good."

"Jon, have you read some books that you liked this year?"

"Yeah, a few."

I know that Jon has recommended *Soldier's Heart* and *Love That Dog* to some of his friends in class, so I can tell that he values at least some of what he is reading.

"Remember when I told the class that the average adult American read only four books last year? You are reading more than most adults do. Celebrate that, and don't worry so much about requirements. Just keep reading!"

Jon is reading, although not as much as either one of us thinks he should. His participation in our reading community, by recommending the books that he is reading to other readers, reflects growing engagement. The fact that Jon was previously able to get through an entire school year and read only two or three books and that this was acceptable is not a fact I dwell on. What I do honor, however, is his increase in reading. By the end of the year, Jon had, in fact, read twenty-five books and, at least some of the time, had found reading worthwhile.

Traditional Practice: Round-Robin and Popcorn Reading

Round-robin reading is the entrenched practice of calling on students randomly to read aloud. Some teachers use a modern variation of round-robin reading—popcorn reading—in an attempt to add a level of fun to the drudgery of reading aloud. During popcorn reading, the teacher calls on a student, who reads for a determined period of time or text length, and then the first reader calls on another student to pick up where they left off, jumping readers around the room like popcorn in a popper. Read-aloud activities like round-robin and popcorn reading are popular among teachers when the entire class reads the same book, short story, or textbook passage.

By randomly calling on students to read, these methods are meant to ensure that all students are following along, that they are paying attention to what is being read, and that everyone reads aloud occasionally, but I don't think these purposes serve the needs of students. The added factor that students hate round-robin reading makes it an act I question. Ask your adult friends what they remember about reading aloud in this manner, and I'll bet that many recall round-robin reading with the same level of anxiety as that associated with going to the board to solve math problems in front of the class. Under the guise of a fun activity for students, reading aloud on demand is just torture—not only for those who are reading but also for those who are listening.

A Closer Look at Round-Robin Reading

Let's take a look at what is really going on during round-robin reading: Billy is called on to read a section from the social studies textbook. Billy, who is not a strong reader, labors to get through the passage, halting when he comes to words he does not know until he gets prompting from the teacher and, most likely, other students. He is embarrassed by his poor reading ability, and the frustration he senses from the other students. Everyone, including Billy, is relieved when he is done. Billy does not remember much of what he read because he did not understand it, but it doesn't matter. He does not continue to follow along with the class. He has already been called on to read once, and is safe for another day.

I suppose that we could avoid humiliating developing readers by not asking them to read aloud, but the picture is not any better for the capable readers.

Susie, who is a wonderful reader, whips through her section with few problems. The developing readers, who cannot keep up with the pace of Susie's reading, are lost. Even if Susie reads the text fluently, it is likely that some students do not have enough background knowledge of the topic or the vocabulary to comprehend what she is reading. Susie, whose primary goal is to dazzle the class with how much better she reads than Billy, does not pay much attention to what she reads, either. Once she finishes her part, Susie does not follow along with the rest of the class, but reads ahead because she can.

The popcorn popper continues, readers burn out one by one, and comprehension breaks down for everyone in the room.

I can't believe that any teacher, after reflecting on how this method of group reading really plays out in a classroom, would still use it. To assume that all students are following along is false. Think back to episodes when the student who was called on to read was obviously not following along and needed prompting to find the proper place to start. Poor readers dread getting called on to read, and good readers are bored by laboring through the reading of slower, less capable readers than themselves. Round-robin reading does nothing to foster a feeling of reading success in any but the best readers, and it doesn't build anyone's oral reading ability or fluency, either.

Alternative: Prepare and Practice for Oral Reading

It is important for students to practice reading aloud in order to develop confidence and fluent oral reading ability, so how can we encourage students to read aloud, but avoid the negatives of round-robin and popcorn reading?

- *Preview the text before you read it.* Point out to students the features of the text, such as visuals or vocabulary, that students will need to understand in order to comprehend the passage. Determine what they already know about the material, and pre-teach any concepts or vocabulary they do not know but will need for comprehension.

- *Assign students a section to read ahead of time, and give them time to practice reading it.* Reading a piece of text silently a few times will improve students' ability to read the text aloud later. If students can read the text aloud a few times, too, that's even better.

Alternative: Substitutes for Oral Reading

We need to consider whether we are asking students to read orally because we see a benefit for them in this practice or because it is a time-saver or a work saver for the teacher. Reading texts orally as a class takes a huge amount of time that we can little afford to waste on an activity that does not improve students' reading ability. There are better methods for increasing students' fluency than round-robin reading, including share-reading as I suggested earlier in this chapter. Here are some additional ideas:

- *Pair each student with a buddy, and let the two students read the text together.* Choose partners that are close to the same reading ability. Match developing readers or English language learners with students who read on grade level. Do not pair your lowest readers with your most gifted ones. High-ability students resent being used as tutors, and they, too, deserve the ability to grow as readers—something they will not be able to accomplish by reading with readers who are less capable than they are. True, developing readers need the support of a better reader as a model, but giving them a racehorse reader to work with will only feed their sense of reading inadequacy.

- *Use unabridged audiotapes, CDs, or podcasts.* Students will have a fluent reading model to follow along with, and the teacher will not have to read the same text six times in one day. Trust me, my students will tell you that author Gary Soto's Spanish-accented rendition of the song "La Bamba" in his short story of the same name is much better than mine! As students listen to the audio, you can stop the recording at key points in the text or replay sections for discussion purposes. School librarians can often locate audiotapes or CDs for many children's books. Many publishers now include CDs of textbooks in ancillary packages, and online services such as TumbleTalkingBooks (http://www.tumblebooks.com/talkingbooks/) and Audible (www.audible.com) offer a huge selection of book podcasts.

Traditional Practice: Incentive Programs

Shortly after Thanksgiving break, I greet my students with a stack of papers. "Ladies and gentlemen, I have the packets for the Six Flags Reading Contest. You may have participated in this contest before. If you read 360 minutes between now and February 15, you can earn a free student ticket to Six Flags."

Corbin is incredulous: "Three hundred and sixty minutes between now and *February* 15? Mrs. Miller, we will read more than that in a month."

"That's true, Corbin. My feeling is that if you are already doing the reading, you might as well get the free ticket."

Daniel, my entrepreneur, asks, "If we read more, can we get more tickets?"

"No, Daniel, just the one."

Brittany whines, "Do we have to keep that lame log to get the ticket? I don't care about the ticket if I have to keep that log."

"Hey guys, you are already doing the reading. Getting the ticket is a nice bonus, don't you think? I will keep a folder on my desk for the Six Flags logs, and when you complete yours, stick it in the file. I will turn them in to Ms. Taylor [the school librarian] when it is a little closer to the due date." Someone digs out a calculator to see how many days of in-class and nightly reading they have to complete in order to rack up 360 minutes.

"Let's see, if I read at least twenty minutes a day in class and twenty minutes a day at home, it will take me nine days to read 360 minutes. Hey, Mrs. Miller, how much time do we have?"

"Two months or so. I imagine that most of you will be done before winter break."

I am grateful to Six Flags and our librarian for administering a program that promotes reading. I think their goal of rewarding students for reading by giving them a fun day at an exciting theme park is a noble one. What I take issue with is the embarrassingly little amount of reading that students are expected to accomplish over an extended period of time in order to earn a reward. In addition, I have never observed a student who developed a long-term reading habit because of an incentive program. Even if students are somehow motivated to read because of the ticket, free pizza, or other prize, odds are that they will abandon reading as soon as the incentive is earned. Unfortunately, the only purpose these programs serve is to convince students there is no innate value in reading and that it is only worth doing if there is a prize attached.

Alternative: Reading Bestows Gifts on the Reader

I want my students to learn what life readers know: reading is its own reward. Reading is a university course in life; it makes us smarter by increasing our vocabulary and background knowledge of countless topics. Reading allows us to travel to destinations that we will never experience outside of the pages of a book. Reading is a way to find friends who have the same problems we do and who can give advice on solving those problems. Through reading, we can witness all that is noble, beautiful, or horrifying about other human beings. From a book's characters, we can learn how to conduct ourselves. And most of all, reading is a communal act that connects you to other readers, comrades who have traveled to the same remarkable places that you have and been changed by them, too.

Rewarding reading with prizes cheapens it, and undermines students' chance to appreciate the experience of reading for the possibilities that it brings to their life. For students who read a lot, these programs are neither an incentive, nor a challenge. Yes, my classes participate in the schoolwide incentive programs when they are offered; after all, they would blaze past the requirements anyway. But I never let my students lose sight of what the true prize is; an appreciation of reading will add more to their life than a hundred days at Six Flags ever could.

End-of-Year Evaluations

SCHOOL IS OUT FOR THE YEAR, and several altruistic students are spending their first day of vacation helping me move into my new classroom. Melinda, a former student who is now in high school, shows up to help, like she does every summer, and supervises the less-experienced volunteers. Carting boxes of books and dragging bookcases down the hall, I briefly contemplate whether I have too many books and then quickly discard this notion. Can you ever have too many books?

Turning my attention to my desk, I sift through the neatly clipped and stacked piles of forms I still need to file. I grab one stack to take home and read—my students' end-of-year surveys, in which they filled out a questionnaire that I designed to identify how students have grown as readers during the school year (see Figure 6.3). Reading through these surveys later, I consider my students' personal feelings about reading, whether they met their reading goals, their favorite books and genres, and their heartfelt opinions about reading response letters, genre requirements, and in-class reading time. Data from these surveys shows amazing growth in the volume of reading my students did and a marked change in their attitudes toward reading in general.

On their reading surveys from the first week of school, my fifty-four students reported reading 939 books in fifth grade, an

End of the Year Reading Evaluation

Directions: Please answer the following questions in as much detail as possible. I want to read
your honest thoughts and opinions about reading and the design of this class.

1.   What is your attitude towards reading? Has this class changed your opinion? If so,
how?

As you know, my feelings towards reading before this class here not good ones, (large in part to "class reading") But now I, I love it more than my brother. SKILL,

2.   Estimate how many books you read INDEPENDENTLY last school year:

0, zip, nada.

3.   How many books did you read independently this year (include all of the books that
you read even if they did not meet genre requirements)?

about 70 - 75 (they all probably aren't on my reading log cause I forgot.

4.   How do you feel about the amount of reading you did this year?

I'd say an increase of about 70 books is pretty good for one year so I feel pretty good about myself.

5.   Did you meet your genre requirements? If not, explain.

Yes, although I might have not wrote them all down in my reading log.

6.   What was the best book you read this year? Why?

Inkspill!!! Not only was it a great book, but racing Kenan to see who could finish it first added to the excitment.

7.   Which topics, authors, series, books, etc. do you plan to read in the future?

I guarentee that I will buy Inkdeath the day it comes out, I also know that there will be more Cliane books so I'll buy these to

FIGURE 6.3: *One Student's Feedback, Shown on Evaluation Form*
Source: *Michelle, grade 6.*

8. What do you wish you had learned about reading this year that you did not?

Ummm.... nothing really. I probably learned more this year than the last two years combined.

9. What advice can you give readers in this class next year?

Listen to Mrs. Miller's book recomdatious. She is the Great Power.

10. In the next section, put a checkmark next to the elements of this class that have helped you as a reader. Circle which factor was most important to you.

classroom library ✓

school librarian/library

book commercials

independent reading time in class ✓

nightly reading time at home ✓

conferences ✓
(maybe)

teacher who reads ✓✓ ✓✓

conversations with classmates ✓
(maybe)

book club

reading response letters ✓

read alouds

book reviews

OTHER: _____

11. If you were designing the layout of the classroom library and the checkout system, what would you do to make it easier for students to use?

I though it was pretty easy to use this year exept for the whole checkout-card thing. I haven't wrote on that thing for 3 months.

FIGURE 6.3: *(Continued)*

average of 17 books per student; twenty-four students had read 5 or fewer books the entire year. During sixth grade, the same group read 3,332 books, an average of 62 books per student. The least number of books read by any student was 22. Students' attitudes about how much reading they did ranged from disbelief to amazement to pride. Bongani was so proud of the number of books he read that he photocopied his reading log to show to relatives. With great drama Ben claimed, "I feel reborn!" and Mathew, who had read 0 books in fifth grade and 40 in sixth, remarked, "I read more than I thought I would in a lifetime!"

Of the factors that students identified as contributing the most to their increased motivation and interest in reading, in-class reading time was selected as a significant factor by all fifty-four. Fifty chose our classroom library, and forty-six commented that having a teacher who reads helped them develop as readers themselves. I was surprised, in light of the fact that our class had no home reading requirement, that forty-two students indicated that they spent more time reading at home than they did before entering my class. This information reinforced my belief that students who read more at school are more likely to continue reading at home.

I use students' feedback as a tool to identify which components of our reading workshop need a tweak for next year. Book reviews, which I implemented halfway through the school year, were not as helpful as I had hoped they would be in sparking readers' interest. I think if we had begun writing reviews earlier in the year, they would have worked better because students would rely on them more than they did when we only created a few. The same goes for the after-school book club, which did not get off the ground until February.

Through this survey, students celebrate their reading accomplishments, express their opinions to me one more time about the structure of our class, and set future reading goals. By visualizing and stating plans for reading after my class, I hope that students will continue to move forward as readers. I tell them, "The most important books you will ever read are those you choose to read this summer. By continuing to read, you will prove that you are readers now without the requirement from me to do so."

CHAPTER 7

Letting Go

Until I feared I would lose it, I never loved to read.
One does not love breathing.

—Harper Lee

I realize that I will probably never have the opportunity to read as much as I do now in class ever again.

—Michelle

TO PARAPHRASE Gary Schmidt's *The Wednesday Wars*, one of my new favorites: teachers plant in the fall and harvest in the spring. Looking around my classroom this March day, I know it to be true. My students are bent over their books; one even reads while blowing his nose and walking to the trash can. I end the year in the same way that I began it: sitting in my green chair, reading. Not reading in front of them as much as reading with them. I wonder, sometimes, whether I have pulled my students into a circle around me or whether they have opened their circle, and allowed me to come into it. Whichever it is, reading is what we are about now, and we are happy doing it.

Instead of following me around, begging for book recommendations, my students have started to make preview stacks and suggest books to each other. They are mimicking what I have modeled. They don't need me to support them as readers as much as they did in August, and this thought warms me and makes me sad at the same time. I know that they will be leaving me soon. For me, the worst part about being a teacher is saying good-bye to children whom I have loved, many of whom I will never see again. All I will have are the mental snapshots I take of them now, peeking over my book.

Alex is a reading bonfire, and our library and the time to read have been kindling for him. He is so consumed by reading that he tunes everything out, including even me at times. I hope I am not the only teacher he will have who does not mind.

If you have a book with a dog in it, give it to Melissa. Don't give sad books to Parker; she claims to hate them, although she seems to read a lot of them.

Molly loves suspenseful, fast-paced books and is very picky about what she reads. I have given her twenty books to preview at one time, and she has walked away without one. Selecting books she will like has become a personal challenge for me. I see a future in publishing for her.

Kenan and Michelle are head to head at their opposing desks, dueling to see who will finish *Inkheart* first. It appears that Kenan left his copy at home today and is reading something else. The lead, for now, goes to Michelle.

Bethany, Madison, and Dana are so enamored with Scott Westerfeld's Midnighters series that they have convinced me to use tridecalogisms, the thirteen-letter words that have such power over the darklings in the books, for our next vocabulary list (see Figure 7.1). They bring me new words each day. Instead of our usual ten words, this particular list will have thirteen.

Brandon, who had never been an expert in anything but getting into trouble before arriving in my class, is now the class expert in all things Gary Paulsen. When our new copies of *The River* and *Brian's Hunt* arrived, he stood at my desk and waited for me to cover them with Con-Tact paper so he could take them home. I knew when I ordered them that Brandon would get them first.

If Margaret Peterson Haddix has written a book Jordan hasn't read, I haven't found it. It is probably a good thing that the end of the year is close. I have almost run out of suggestions for her.

Daniel is lugging so many books home in his backpack to read over spring break that I worry he will have back trouble. He asks me every day if I have finished *Children of the Lamp: Day of the Djinn Warriors*, so he can read it next.

Josh and Riley, confident and popular, claim not to be readers, but both have quietly put more books into the hands of their

FIGURE 7.1: *Madison's homemade locker tag shows her love for Midnighters.*

classmates than almost anyone. They are proof that if you can get the cool kids to read, others will follow.

Bishop has so much enthusiasm for the books he loves that you can't help catching it. I credit him with making *Drums, Girls, and Dangerous Pie* the most widely read book in class this year, despite the fact that we own just one copy of it.

We tease Bongani and Betenia about all of the book hostages they have. They are both so book-hungry that they collect mounds of books in their locker as if they were storing nuts for winter.

And I have to wonder, is a reading winter coming for them soon? I recognize how tenuous their newfound love of reading is and how few teachers let students run wild as readers like I do.

I know this because some of them come back and tell me.

Back to Square One?

Ally and her twin, Hanna, show up in my doorway shortly after school begins to return the books they borrowed from me over the summer. The twins are talkative and bubbly, as usual, and we spend a few minutes chatting about what they did during the break. Our conversation drifts to the books they are returning and the twins' impressions of them, but the talk eventually turns to their current seventh-grade English class.

Ally sighs, "I am heartbroken, Mrs. Miller. Our new teacher doesn't believe in giving us free reading time."

"Really?" I am walking a line here. I want to acknowledge Ally's feelings without maligning the teacher she will have for the entire year.

"She has all of these books that we are required to read as a class, but we don't get any time to read our own books."

Hanna chimes in: "Yeah, we are all reading *The Westing Game*, and it is so boring."

I would never have recommended Raskin's mystery *The Westing Game* to Ally in a million years. It is not her type of book. She is a fantasy gal through and through. The fact that the book is several years below her reading level is a mark against it, as well. I can see that we are back where we started: teacher-required reading and novel units without any thought to students' interests or reading level. It is insulting that Ally's reading experiences go unacknowledged by her new teacher. Her reading level and vocabulary development won't progress much if she is reading books that are too easy for her.

"We have to keep our books in a plastic Ziploc bag because she doesn't think we can take care of them. She told us that she knows we probably don't read enough, and that she wants to make sure we read more. Doesn't she know where we came from? We all read tons last year, and she treats us like we don't read."

Dismayed, I blurt out, "Did you tell her? Did you tell her that you read like crazy last year?"

"No, it wouldn't make any difference to her." I don't know whether this is true, but what is clear is that Ally and Hanna are underground readers whose feelings about reading and prolific reading experience have no place in their English class. Both girls developed a love of reading in my class, and I hate to think that they will have to pursue this love outside of school in order to maintain it. We are back to square one. Instilling lifelong reading habits in my students is like trying to hold the ocean back with a broom, a futile endeavor, if they are going to go right back to the same controlling environment they had before my class.

Ally and Hanna leave that day with new books to read, of course. But they will have to read those books at home. I am thrilled that the girls came back to see me, but crestfallen because they are not going to get any reading time in school this year—other than for their assigned books—and because there is nothing, absolutely nothing I can do about it. I wish I could talk to their teacher, but there is no way that I could question another teacher about what she does in her classroom.

I do the only thing I can do: get in my car and cry the entire drive home. I ask myself, would my students be better off if they had never had me as a teacher? (Dramatic wallowing, I know, but I was worked up.) Those plastic bags are a symbol that reading is an act students cannot take responsibility for without monitoring from a teacher. Why do we work so hard to build fences between our students and books? I may be setting them on the road to life reading, but I am not preparing them for years of traditional, teacher-controlled reading instruction after my class. What's worse, my former students know what they are missing and they are heartbroken about it. They know that reading can be different, and that classrooms can be a place where readers get to choose, where time to read their own books happens every day, and the teacher turns the keys over to students. After talking to the twins, it seems to me that the only way they can survive as enthusiastic readers after my class is to take their reading habits underground.

What Are We Preparing Students for?

I have been told many times, both to my face and through comments on my blog, that I am not preparing my students for the "real world" by letting them read whatever they want. Yes, it's true, if the real world means years of comprehension worksheets and test practice. If those things constitute reading instruction, then I suppose the naysayers are right, I am not preparing them.

Why should I subject students to negative experiences now in order to prepare them for negative experiences later? I just don't think mindless work is what I should be grooming them for. I grow weary of hearing teachers say, "We have to get them ready for seventh grade, or high school, or college." They are in sixth grade! What about having an enriching, powerful, glorious year in sixth grade? The purpose of school should not be to prepare students for more school. We should be seeking to have fully engaged students now.

If that argument is not enough for you, then consider the evidence from free-reading classrooms like mine. Allowing students to choose their own books and control most of their own decisions about their reading, writing, and thinking does a better job of preparing them for literate lives than the traditional—and ubiquitous—novel units, test practices, and pointless projects. What are we waiting for?

Richard Allington's findings from thirty years ago indicated that students weren't spending enough time actually *reading* during reading instruction, and they still aren't. The title alone of Allington's landmark article "If They Don't Read Much, How They Ever Gonna Get Good?" tells me everything I need to know. That article was published in 1977, the year before I entered middle school. I certainly didn't see more reading in my middle school classroom as a result of this research, and I don't see it in many classrooms now. No matter what intervention strategies you employ to support developing readers or what enrichment projects you provide to your most gifted ones, none of it is going to affect the reading achievement of all of the students in your classroom the way hours and hours of time spent reading will.

Scores of research findings, federal policy documents, and books from gurus tell teachers that actual reading is the most valuable classroom activity. Although I read a lot of research, you don't have to look any further than the catalogues and magazines the average teacher receives in the mail. Thumbing through the International Reading Association's Professional Development catalogue, I count seven books whose explicit focus is to promote independent reading and students' choices in reading material. If I add the books that advocate giving students some choice—for example, through literature circles—or the books that recommend independent reading as part of a comprehensive teaching model, I count fifteen more. The March 2008 issue of *Book Links*, a publication from the American Library Association, includes an article on motivating readers with the subheading "Sparking Student Interest" and an editorial from a teacher calling for a national initiative to connect students with books instead of focusing on testing.

Despite the abundant information available on implementing free-choice reading programs and the clear research support for such practices, why is so little authentic reading done in schools? When students do get to read a book, why is the book still weighed down with so much "stuff," as Allington calls it, instead of reading? I think it is acculturation. Teachers do what everyone else is doing. How can you plan and collaborate with other teachers if you see reading differently than they do? How are you going to get materials if your department head will not order them for you? How do you justify thirty minutes a day of independent reading for your students if your principal does not understand the value of such a practice?

Even if teachers feel that letting their students read is more effective than any other practice in developing their capacity as strong readers, there is little institutional support for independent reading—that is, true independent reading without skill-based programs, comprehension tests, test practices, or incentives tied to it. There is a powerful pull from colleagues and administrators to keep doing it the old way.

I still panic when other language arts teachers administer a complete practice test for the Texas state reading assessment to their students in order to build their "endurance" for the actual test in two months, wondering whether I should be doing it, too. The week of the practice test, a colleague told me, "My students can't sit through six hours of testing and focus to the end. I tell them that I wouldn't ask them to run a marathon without running a few miles first." I think that it shouldn't take a capable reader six hours to complete a reading test and that the best method for building up reading miles is to read books, but my opinion sticks in my throat and stays there.

Fighting the Culture

It is hard to fight the culture even when what you see in your classroom every day tells you that you are getting it right. And I am getting it right, I know it. My students' test scores are as high as or higher than those of every class in the schools where I have taught.

This is not data to brag about unless the state's minimum standards for students' performance are your only goal. Admittedly, I breathe a sigh of relief each year when my students' test scores come back, just like everyone else.

Why do I still feel this way, even though I have years of classroom data to prove that reading freedom has a powerful impact on reading achievement and mountains of research to back them up? It is the culture of teacher-centered instruction and standardized testing hysteria. The culture makes me question myself, and I know that it is the reason why many teachers resist altering their practice. After all, these teacher-centered methods of teaching reading appear to be effective except for the small detail that children learn to hate reading. There is a fear of diverging from what is working because doing something new with students might not work, and who can take that chance when our reputations as teachers and, possibly, our jobs are on the line?

But this culture is exactly why we have to take that chance and give reading back to students in every manner that we can. The institutional focus on testing and canned programs drains every ounce of joy from reading that students have or will have in the future. We have turned reading into a list of "have to's," losing sight of the reality that students *and adults* are more motivated by "want to's." The have to's of reading—the test practice, the skill instruction, the literary analysis—are part of what we must teach students; I am not arguing that point. Students need to know how to take a reading test, break down a piece of literature, and read a textbook. I teach those concepts, just like you, but all of the skill-based reading instruction in the world will not stick with students if they are never expected or allowed to practice reading with books. And that kind of instruction is a guarantee that most of them will never read, not in the summer, not at home, and *never again* when their formal schooling ends.

Learning from Exemplars

Before I became a teacher, I was a bookkeeper. I worked in hotel and restaurant management for a decade. While I attest that a lot of what I needed to know about teaching reading I learned through my habit of lifelong reading, I picked up a tip or two from my corporate experiences. When corporate leaders desire to improve the efficiency, productivity, or earnings of their companies, they look at what the exemplars in their industry are doing and plan out methods for copying the procedures and attitudes that make those exemplars successful.

The trend in education today is toward data-based decision making, a practice that was also borrowed from the corporate world. States compare their data: test scores, graduation rates, college-readiness statistics, and so on. School districts compare their data with those of other districts, and schools compare their data with those of other schools. Despite the increased use of concrete data to drive instructional decisions and the efforts of scores of researchers to define the best methods for increasing reading achievement, many teachers teach reading the same way that their predecessors did thirty years ago.

These data comparisons help education administrators plan how to spend resources or hire and train teachers, but they don't help teachers determine what they should do every morning when students show up for class. Instead of looking for answers to our instructional questions outside of our classrooms, I believe that we should be looking inside of our classrooms and learning from our own students. Our exemplars for performance exist in our classrooms. What do the best readers know about reading that the developing ones don't? What can we learn from our best readers to inform decision making about our poorest ones?

Hands down, the students who read the most are the best at every part of school—reading, writing, researching, content-specific knowledge, all of it (Krashen, 2004). They are the best test takers, too. Teachers know this. Successful, strong readers are the ones teachers don't worry about, the ones who could pass the state test on the first day of class, and need their books to educate themselves while sitting in our classes all year, learning nothing new from us. Instead of leaving these students to simmer on the back burner while we struggle to educate our poor readers, why not teach all of our students to adopt the attitudes and behaviors of the best readers?

Lifelong Readers Are the Goal

We make it hard on ourselves, that's certain. It's hard to give up the control. After all, if we are not micromanaging every aspect of reading for students, can we call what we are doing teaching? To give up control, you have to change your mind-set about what teaching is, what it can be for you, not just your students. I am still learning how to let go. One realization I have come to is that there is a marked difference between managing a classroom and controlling it. I can manage my classroom without dictating all thought and decision making for my students. My students' self-concept as readers must extend beyond the classroom, even my classroom, or they have gained nothing lasting from me. If teachers control reading, we never give ownership of it to students. Students will not walk out of our classrooms with internal motivation to read if they see reading as an act that takes place only in school under the control of their teachers. Reading ultimately belongs to readers, not schools, and not schoolteachers.

There are too many adults who equate reading with school; some take pride in not having read a book since graduation. This is not just the case for poor readers. This is true of most readers, even those who passed our classes and state assessments year after year. No teacher I know thinks this sorry state is acceptable, yet we fail to take responsibility for it, blaming parents for not encouraging their children to read, and the students themselves for not wanting to.

I want more for my students than this nonreading state. I want them to feel that reading is a pursuit in which they continue to learn and receive solace and joy throughout their life. I want what *English Journal* editor and columnist Chris Crowe wants for his own children when he begs, "I'd like just once, to have one of them stagger into the kitchen, bleary-eyed and late for breakfast, because of staying up all night to finish a novel. I'd love to see them curled up on the couch rereading a favorite book. I would go to my grave a contented old man if once before I die, and before my kids grow up, I could hear one of my children talking excitedly to a friend about a book just finished." This entreaty was not an admonishment directed toward his children or a missive from an expert; this was a dad pleading with his children's teachers to encourage his kids to read.

Connecting Through Books

My journey with students takes me back to myself and what I have always known about reading. Being a reader is how I choose to spend my life, every aspect of it, inside and outside of the classroom. I often wonder whether my identity as a reader, someone who reads voraciously and always has a book recommendation, is all I have to offer. That may be true, but it is an oversimplification. How can I express the extent to which reading has shaped who I am as a human being?

Although I see myself as kind, I am not a demonstrative person. If I have ever brought you a book unasked for, know that I cared. I said everything to you that I wanted to with that book. I have enough wisdom to acknowledge that an author's words are more eloquent than my own. When we meet and I discover that we have read and loved the same books, we are instant friends. We know a great deal about each other already if we both read. I imagine this is why I strive so hard to get people around me to read. If you don't read, I don't know how to communicate with you. I know this is a shortcoming. Perhaps my mother, who worried that reading would make me socially stunted, was half right. I can never express who I really am in my own words as powerfully as my books can.

This is how I show my students that I love them—by putting books in their hands, by noticing what they are about, and finding books that tell them, "I know. I know. I know how it is. I know who you are, and even though we may never speak of it, read this book, and know that I understand you." We speak in this language of books passing back and forth, books that say, "You are a dreamer; read this." "You are hurting inside; read this." "You need a good laugh; read this."

The time students spend in my class is fleeting, over too soon or, perhaps, just in time, but the hours we have spent together reading will outlast a school year. Books are immortality for writers, and as the conduit through which books have flowed into the hands of so many children, I feel that books are my immortality, too. If my students remember my class as the year they devoured scores of books, then that has to be enough for me. I cannot control what happens after they leave my class, but I do wonder, is it enough for them? Considering how many of my former students still e-mail me for book recommendations or show up in my doorway years later to talk about books, I would say it's not.

And They Do Return

It is Friday afternoon, the book club my students begged me to start has just ended, and I am cleaning up my room. I look up from the desk I am clearing off to see Matthew standing in the doorway. Beaming, he announces, "The smell, I love the smell of this room. I can't describe it; it's like new books and cleaner. How are you, Mrs. Miller?"

I give him a little hug, noticing that he has grown since last spring when he left my class. We spend the next half hour catching up on the books we have read since last summer. He asks, "Did you read *Gregor and the Code of Claw*?" (Spoiler alert: If you haven't read it yet, you might want to skip the next six sentences!)

"Yes I did. The ending suggests that the series might not be over. I still think there is something about that neighbor that Suzanne Collins did not tell us."

"Yeah, I know what you mean. I can't believe she killed off Ares. He was one of the best characters! Did you know that *The Battle of the Labyrinth* is coming out soon?"

I interrupt, "May 6! I wonder how Riordan's going to weave the Minotaur myth into this one."

"Hey, Michael and I signed up to take mythology next year."

"Matthew, you could teach that class! Think about all of the mythology you read last year."

Matthew helps me stack chairs and pick up trash while we talk and talk about books. It is nice that we can fall back into talking about books so easily when we have not seen each other for eight months, further proof that Matthew and I are connected as readers long after my role as his teacher passes. We catch up on all of the series we are following and rehash our impressions of *Harry Potter and the Deathly Hallows*. I tell Matt about the movies based on *Inkheart* and *Uglies* that are coming out soon. I show him the new feline-fantasy Warriors books that I snagged from a book sale. (Ally, Hanna, and Matt had begged me to buy the books the spring before.) Matt reveals, "I buy books all of the time. I spend all of my money at Barnes & Noble." Our conversation starts to reveal more disturbing facts about the health of reading beyond my classroom.

"Matthew, why don't you go to the school library?"

"My teacher never takes us to the library. The only way I can go is before or after school, and I am always rushing. Whenever I find a book I like there, it is the third in a series or something, and they never have the first one. They don't promote reading over there [at the middle school] the way that you did.'' He sighs, ''Well, no one promotes reading like you.''

I wind up digging through the class library to find Matthew some books to read that I know he did not read last year, teasing him, ''Well, I guess it's manipulative of me, but if I loan you some books to read, you will have to come back and see me to return them.''

Matthew's dramatic declaration that ''no one'' promotes reading the way I do may not be completely accurate, but he only has the *eight teachers* he's had since kindergarten to go on. Providing students with piles of books to choose from and giving them time to read them seems too easy, but it works, and I am not the only adult invested in motivating children to read who knows it. A sampling of comments on my blog entries bears this out.

Why we should validate students' interests when recommending books and using them in class:

> If we want children who are avid and excited readers, we need to let them read what interests them.
>
> —*Donna Green, posted March 13, 2008*

How spending more time assessing students and less time reading beats all the joy for reading out of them:

> It is sad how illustrating the importance of reading and writing (through testing) has come at the expense of the passion some kids have for it.
>
> —*Jason, posted February 29, 2008*

Why the best reading program is still the first reading program most children encounter while sitting on a parent's lap—connecting with books and spending time reading:

> Providing kids with lots and lots of interesting books and time in which to read them seems too low-tech, too easy, too lacking in rigor. Of course it can't possibly work.
>
> —*Erin, posted February 13, 2008*

Why reading is about the children and the books, not the programs and the teacher:

> As an English teacher at an alternative high school, I have seen many students who are non-readers become motivated to read simply through having the opportunity to choose their own books. In my view it is vital for our students to have easy access to books to which they can relate. When students find such books, they suddenly can't put them down. I love when this happens.
>
> —*Terry, posted February 15, 2008*

These pockets of reading zealotry are not enough, and we all know that these teachers are not in the majority. We should not have to become underground teachers. Something has to change. Students should not have to suffer. Every time they pick up a book, we punish them with overused worksheets and unending analysis and discussions. Why would they ever choose to read on their own? There needs to be more of us, and we need to get a lot louder about telling our administrators, colleagues, and parents what we believe. Of course, we have to believe that students need to read more and have more control over their reading in the first place.

Until that happens, I will still get e-mails like this one from Kelsey's mother:

> This is a big TAKS [Texas Assessment of Knowledge and Skills] year for Kelsey. Can you give me some advice on what we should do to help her pass? I know you are busy with your students, but you seemed to reach Kelsey.

Yes, the same Kelsey who triumphantly passed the TAKS in sixth grade, the year I taught her. Her mother is worried about the TAKS again, and has to contact me to get advice? Am I the last teacher who reached her, two years ago?

The students trickle back to me in pairs, and send me e-mails begging for lists or to find someone, anyone, who cares about the latest installment in the Clique series. It is touching, and I miss them all. It is gratifying to know that I have had an impact on them to such a degree, and that they are still reading. They shouldn't have to struggle so much to remain readers, though. It is heartbreaking that their reading communities have not expanded or evolved since sixth grade. I know that without dedicated class time to read or a community of reading peers to support them, some stop reading. The experiences with reading that I share with my students are that fragile.

Read all of the books on teaching you want, even this one, but my most recent e-mail from Ally, who spent all of seventh grade in a teacher-controlled reading environment, says it all:

> Mrs. _____ has given us a reading assignment with books we actually WANT to read! I never thought it was possible. . . . She is having us choose from books like *The Sands of Time, The Book of Story Beginnings, The Sea of Trolls* (I chose this one), and *Code Orange.* For once I can read a book in her class that is enjoyable.

It took seven months for Ally's classroom to get back to the first day of sixth grade. Students will read if we give them the books, the time, and the enthusiastic encouragement to do so. If we make them wait for the one unit a year in which they are allowed to choose their own books to become readers, they may choose never to read at all. To keep our students reading, we have to let them.

Afterword

READING IS FUNDAMENTAL. Growing up in the late 1960s and early 1970s, I heard these words on a public-service television spot, squeezed between my favorite TV shows, *Bonanza* and *The Big Valley*. Spoken by a young boy of ten or eleven—someone close to my age—those words were a call to action. I got the message that if I ever expected to know more about the world around me, I would need to read. Living in rural Oklahoma, my access to books was limited to the small local library and the picked-over shelves of my school's classrooms. The encouragement and necessity that lived within this boy's voice stayed with me. His was a message that reading could offer me the opportunity of knowing about other people and places. And I never forgot it.

At the time, America was experiencing roiling political change—the civil rights movement, the Vietnam War, the resignation of a president. I saw reading as social engagement, a path to understanding this revolution—the ideas, the challenges, and the people. Reading was instrumental for me in exploring life far from my rural Oklahoma childhood. I was fortunate. I believed that I could be a part of something greater by reading. As a practicing school principal today, it is my duty to create an atmosphere that sends that same message to students. I must find teachers who believe that reading is a vehicle that allows students to travel beyond their classroom walls.

Yet how clearly are we sending the "reading is fundamental" message to our young people today? Are the students in our public school classrooms experiencing reading as a means to reflect on the world? I hope so, but I am also skeptical. Our national discussion of reading has been reduced to a talking point, a measurement score. How can we get our students to open books and start reading when, in many classrooms, the focus is on test performance? I believe in and support the idea that teachers and schools should be accountable for students' performance, but I fear that we on the inside, who work in public schools, are misrepresenting the fundamental idea of reading. Reading is more than a number. It is a civic responsibility—one that should live in and outside the classroom. And teachers and schools play a critical role in keeping this message on track.

By creating this sense of responsibility within our students, we are preparing them to be informed decision makers and contributors to our communities. If we create a passion for reading within our students, they will be able to carry on the kind of inquiry that is needed to function in our democracy. Our students are shortchanged if we fail to teach reading beyond the narrow definition of a test score. Our students are shortchanged if the fundamental message of reading is captured only in an encouraging word on a poster or an impersonal voice in a public-service announcement. We who work with children every day in schools across America have an obligation to live the reading life ourselves.

We must believe that reading is fundamental for ourselves, for our students, for all students in order to help promote the ideas that will carry each of us forward. Reading must lead our agenda as public school teachers and administrators, not in a way that is narrowly defined but in a way that helps students discover their own sense of purpose. Whether these young readers are from a booming metropolis or a rural community thousands of miles away, we can help them envision other possibilities through the words of E. L. Konigsburg, E. B. White, or Harper Lee.

Donalyn Miller believes that teachers and school administrators are obligated to create powerful reading classrooms. Donalyn Miller believes that students are more than test takers. Donalyn Miller believes that all students are readers, that students must lead sustained reading lives well past their school years. Hers is an important voice that carries the message that reading is fundamental every day in her classroom.

Won't you join the book whisperer movement? By doing so, we will send a thunderous message that reading is critical not only for the welfare of our students but also for the continued health of our democracy. We will empower our students to sustain themselves and our nation. I challenge you to join this reading revolution, to do your part as a public school educator in the United States. Our children cannot afford our silence.

Ron D. Myers, Ph.D.

Principal

Trinity Meadows Intermediate School

Keller, Texas

Appendix A: The Care and Feeding of a Classroom Library

THE SMALL THREE-SHELF, PARTICLEBOARD BOOKCASE that I started with the first year I taught is still a part of my classroom, but it has been relegated to holding archived lesson plans and *The Reading Teacher* journals. The shelves began to bow from holding book tubs a few years ago, and like an old swaybacked horse, it has been put out to pasture. I won't get rid of that shabby, cheap bookcase until it collapses. On days when I despair that I am not accomplishing much with students, that pitiful bookcase reminds me of how far I have come.

When my school, Trinity Meadows Intermediate, opened in 2006, teachers raced to move into their classrooms while construction was still under way. Installing phones in the classrooms, one technician wandered into the office, confused: "Hey, do you want a phone in that library back there?" It took the office staff a few moments to realize that the technician meant my classroom.

To say that my classroom is overflowing with books now would be an understatement. There is no library corner. The whole room is a library corner. My students are literally surrounded by books (see Figure A.1). In fact, we have so many books in the library that all of the large sets of books for share-reading and our after-school book club are shoved in a closet across the hall. When a guest came to my

FIGURE A.1: *Our Classroom Library*
Source: Hope Myers, grade 6.

classroom for a visit, my students and I stuffed several crates of books into cabinets in the workroom across the hall because there was no room under my computer table for them. I felt as if I were hiding dirty laundry from my mother-in-law, afraid that my guest would not understand our need to have piles of books all over the place.

Books Everywhere You Look

Plastic bookcases full of fiction line the walls and wrap around the entire room. These shelves contain rows and rows of plastic shoe boxes. I buy these from discount stores when bins are on sale for a dollar apiece and leave the lids at the store. Each book bin contains books, covers facing out. Since our class reading requirements are based on genres, the books are grouped that way. I order the books according to the popularity of genres. The bins start with realistic fiction, then fantasy and historical fiction, then science fiction, mystery, traditional literature, and, finally, poetry. Every few bins sports a computer-generated bookplate with the genre on it as a guide for students who are looking for books.

The bins are numbered, and every book has a sticker on the cover to match the one on the respective bin. The stickers make it possible for students to reshelve books on their own. Each bin is alphabetical—roughly speaking—within its own genre. If there are not enough books for a particular letter of the alphabet to fill up a bin, one holds several letters. When the bin gets full, I add another bin with the same number, and put the overflow books into it. This way, I do not have to renumber all the books whenever our library expands. We have over 100 bins in the class library now.

Milk crates full of nonfiction are stacked on the floor, with science titles in one; history titles in a second; general nonfiction, including how-to books and advice titles in a third; and biographies, autobiographies, and memoirs in a fourth.

Hardcover books don't fit well in plastic shoe boxes; wider than the bin and too heavy, they tip the bins over. One tall wooden bookcase by the windows holds all of the hardcovers in rows two books deep. This bookcase is not in any order, and students cannot see the covers, but I have to make this concession in order to fit all of the books into it. There are a few students who prefer discovering books pulled at random from a bookshelf. I suppose this crazy-quilt assortment meets that need.

One large bookcase by the door holds dictionaries, thesauri, atlases, and other reference books for writing and social studies. The cabinet at the bottom of this shelf holds audiotapes, headphones, and the cataloguing supplies our class librarians and I need to run the library.

Each student in my classes, as well as other library guests, keeps a library card in a file box. When readers check out a book, they record the title, then check off the book when they return it. I use the same cards that librarians use in book pockets for recording due dates. They are available from a library supply company.

As we get more books, I take more personal items or books on pedagogy home to make more room. (Let's not go into my book situation there!) I hide teaching manuals and ancillaries for textbooks away in cabinets behind my desk. I still use them, but I don't want them to take precedence over the books I read with students. Books we will read together; picture books I use to model lessons; delicate, easily damaged books like our Robert Sabuda pop-ups; and novelty books like *Dragonology* and *Egyptology* I keep behind my desk in built-in shelves.

Acquiring Books

I have purchased every book in our class library with my own money. I cringe a bit admitting that, but I have my reasons. There is not enough money available in school budgets for teachers to develop such extensive libraries. (I talk to many teachers who claim they cannot implement a free-choice reading program in their classroom because they don't have enough books.)

There are personal reasons for me to amass my own collection, too. I am a bit free with my book loans, passing out books to former students, siblings of students, and other teachers, some not even at my school. I have the freedom to do this because these books are mine, and I can loan my books to anyone I want to. If the books in my room were school property, I would never do this, of course. If they were, it would take herculean efforts for me to keep track of the number of books I loan out, and I just cannot devote this much effort to tracking every single book in my room. Yes, books wander off, some for years, but a lot of them wander back. Books from former students wash up in my school mailbox, literary messages-in-a-bottle, with notes apologizing for keeping the books for so long tucked inside.

Furthermore, if I were to change campuses, my library would go with me. No matter what materials I lacked at the new school, I could do without as long as I had my library. This was the case when I changed schools in 2006. I did not have textbooks on the first day of school, but it did not matter; I had my books.

I am not advocating that you purchase books for your own class library, but all teachers spend money on their classroom at one time or another. I never invested in decorations for my classroom; the windows don't have curtains, and there are no motivational posters papering the walls. I chide my students to pick up every pencil they find in the hall so we can have more books!

I do, however, employ methods for getting books that stretch every dollar. I scrounge books from book swaps, discount bookstores, and sales. I often purchase books from garage sales, where books are not big sellers. I frequently walk away with a box of books by offering the seller a few dollars to take the box away. I cull out the books that are worth adding to the library, and take the rest to a book swap later. My students and I buy books from book order companies, who give the ordering teacher points toward purchasing new books. Instead of holiday and teacher appreciation gifts, I encourage students to donate a book to the class library. Students bring me books that they or their siblings don't want anymore, too. I honor the benefactors by designing a computer-generated bookplate with the student's name and the year they were in my class on it.

Caring for Books

When making new additions to the library, there are a few things that must be done to the books before they are available for checkout by students. I stamp every book with my name in two places, once inside the cover and once on the outside edge of the pages. I purchased a self-inking stamp from an office supply store for $15. It lasted five years before I had to get it re-inked. Based on the number of books that find their way back to me from the hall, the school library, and other classrooms, the money for this stamp was well spent.

The majority of our books are paperbacks because they are more affordable, but they do not hold up well. In order to extend the life of the library collection, I cover almost every new or used paperback with clear Con-Tact shelf paper, which you can purchase from a big box or discount store such as Wal-Mart. I trim the edges into flaps and fold them around the corners of the book the same way you would cover a textbook with a paper book cover. The vinyl strengthens and protects the book cover from creasing, tearing, and spills. Library supply catalogs sell rigid plastic adhesive-backed covers, but they are expensive, and for classroom use, they're not significantly better than the vinyl. Covering the books is labor-intensive, so I weigh the cost of the book against the labor and material cost of covering it. If I spent less than a dollar on the book, I just stamp it and put it in the library.

I teach my students how to take care of books. I talk to them about propping books open on the spines, describing how the glue breaks and the pages fall out after a while. I also ask them not to dog-ear books by folding the corners over to mark their place, encouraging them to use a bookmark instead. I used to purchase cute little bookmarks from library supply catalogs, but I decided that was a waste of money. My students often personalize their homemade bookmarks, made from index cards or Post-its, with their names or comments about reading—another tiny way to move reading toward their choices instead of mine.

I do not run the checkout or check-in for our library. In the early days of the year, I explain to students that the freedom to choose books and enjoy such a vast library means they have to take responsibility for keeping the library in shape. When we are choosing class jobs for the year, I pick two or three students from each class to serve as class librarians. The class librarians keep the library organized: applying stickers, stamping, and shelving new books. The librarians also make recommendations and serve as guides, helping their classmates find books when I am busy with other students. All students check out and reshelve their own books.

I am constantly digging in the library—helping students find books and pulling books for recommendations during conferences—but every month or so, I spend some time really looking at the library. Which books are in need of repair? Which books don't seem to get checked out? Unread books are an opportunity for a book pass or a book commercial that will expose them to more readers. Which books have I overlooked when making suggestions to children? Which books should be culled due to damage or long use? I also wipe down the books and the bins with antibacterial wipes every now and then. This job is too gross to expect the class librarians to do, and I want to scrutinize our collection. The library withstands heavy use, and that means a lot of hands come into contact with the books.

Which Books Make the Cut?

How to set up a library like ours may be of some use or interest to you, but the nuts and bolts of library care are secondary to the library questions "Which books do you recommend?" and "What are some of the books that your students like to read?" Although I endorse any student-selected reading material, I am extremely selective about which titles I stock in the classroom library. Space is limited, and I prefer to use the space we have to offer a wide variety of books. In addition, it is my responsibility, not just as a teacher but as a more knowledgeable reader, to lead my students to books that are rich with good writing and well-regarded by reviewers or other readers.

If students' tastes run toward books that have dubious literary merit, they can find these on their own; I cannot pander to their tastes by filling our library with junky books. Is the writing good, or is it schlock? Does the book have interesting social themes, historical information, or language? Award winners, beloved favorites, and books by acclaimed authors dominate our collection. We have few movie, television show, or video game tie-ins in our library; the same goes for series that are basically the same book over and over. I also limit the number of books that reflect popular trends or that are time-sensitive titles like books of lists. The books in our library need to last a long time, and ephemeral pop trends or titles with a short shelf life are luxuries.

There are no adult fiction books in the library, either, even though some of my sixth graders could read them. Eric read Robert Louis Stevenson's horror classic *Dr. Jekyll and Mr. Hyde*, and then moved on to Michael Crichton's adventures *Jurassic Park* and *The Lost World*. Michelle is slowly making her way through her mother's favorite, *Jane Eyre*. I support advanced readers as much as my developing ones, but I am careful about the line between support and providing adult reading materials to eleven-year-olds. Just because a gifted reader can read more advanced texts does not mean that they are emotionally ready for adult themes and issues. This is not my decision to make; it is a parent's decision. Gifted readers should read fiction close to their age level and nonfiction at their advanced reading level (Halsted, 2002). In keeping with this principle, I have gathered college textbooks and adult nonfiction texts on a variety of topics of interest to my students, but I limit the fiction offerings to what is age-appropriate.

The majority of the book choices for our library grow from my own reading experiences and continual recommendations from my network of teachers, librarians, friends, and students. I try to read every book before I place it in the library. Reading a book every few days over summers and holidays, and one book a week during the school year, I rack up about a hundred books a year. Occasionally, I will add an unread book to the library, but only if I have read something else by the author. And I add it to my reading list as soon as possible.

Appendix B: Ultimate Library List

I COULD USE my diverse knowledge of books to create a list for you that would make a killer library. Lord knows a bibliophile like me could spend blissful hours composing it. (It would be an extreme version of the desert island-game!) But in keeping with my beliefs that my students run the reading show in every way possible, I have asked them to create a list for you of the books every teacher, grades five through eight, should have in their class library. I tried to set one hundred books as an arbitrary number for the list, but my students kept those titles coming! Because this list reflects the interests and tastes of real students today, you may not see your favorite authors or treasured books here. Remember item 10 in Pennac's *The Rights of the Reader*: the right not to defend your tastes.

These books are the books the children like to read, not those that a teacher chose for them. I made no attempt to balance reading levels, genres, or topics. The third column of the table indicates titles that have a sequel or are the first in a series. You could expand your library by adding the subsequent titles. Once your students are hooked on a series, they will want to read the rest.

Ultimate Library List (grouped by genre; alphabetical by author)

Title	Author	Sequel or Series?
Realistic Fiction		
Nothing But The Truth	Avi	
Hope Was Here	Bauer, Joan	
Rules of the Road	Bauer, Joan	Yes
Tangerine	Bloor, Edward	
Frindle	Clements, Andrew	
School Story	Clements, Andrew	
The Chocolate War	Cormier, Robert	Yes
Walk Two Moons	Creech, Sharon	
Chasing Redbird	Creech, Sharon	
Seedfolks	Fleischman, Paul	
The Clique	Harrison, Lisi	Yes
The View from Saturday	Konigsburg, E. L.	
The Outcasts of 19 Schuyler Place	Konigsburg, E. L.	
Silent to the Bone	Konigsburg, E. L.	
The Sixth Grade Nickname Game	Korman, Gordon	
Son of the Mob	Korman, Gordon	Yes
Jeremy Fink and the Meaning of Life	Mass, Wendy	
Tripping Over the Lunch Lady	Mercado, Nancy	
Hatchet	Paulsen, Gary	Yes

Title	Author	Sequel or Series?
The Boy Who Saved Baseball	Ritter, John	
The Schwa Was Here	Shusterman, Neal	
Peak	Smith, Roland	
Drums, Girls, and Dangerous Pie	Sonnenblick, Jordan	
Maniac Magee	Spinelli, Jerry	
Loser	Spinelli, Jerry	
Wringer	Spinelli, Jerry	
Stargirl	Spinelli, Jerry	Yes
Surviving the Applewhites	Tolan, Stephanie	
Each Little Bird That Sings	Wiles, Deborah	
Love, Ruby Lavender	Wiles, Deborah	
Fantasy		
The Word Eater	Amato, Mary	
The Underneath	Appelt, Kathi	
Artemis Fowl	Colfer, Eoin	Yes
Gregor the Overlander	Collins, Suzanne	Yes
The Sea of Trolls	Farmer, Nancy	Yes
The Thief Lord	Funke, Cornelia	
Inkheart	Funke, Cornelia	Yes
Princess Academy	Hale, Shannon	
Children of the Lamp	Kerr, P. B.	Yes

Title	Author	Sequel or Series?
Guardians of Ga'Hoole: The Capture	Lasky, Kathryn	Yes
Ella Enchanted	Levine, Gail Carson	
The Lion, the Witch, and the Wardrobe	Lewis, C. S.	Yes
Twilight	Meyer, Stephenie	Yes
Eragon	Paolini, Christopher	Yes
The Lightning Thief	Riordan, Rick	Yes
Harry Potter and the Sorcerer's Stone	Rowling, J. K.	Yes
Midnighters	Westerfeld, Scott	Yes
The Warrior Heir	Chima, Cinda Williams	Yes
The Extraordinary Adventures of Alfred Kropp	Yancey, Rick	Yes

Historical Fiction

Title	Author	Sequel or Series?
Fever 1793	Anderson, Laurie Halse	
The True Confessions of Charlotte Doyle	Avi	
Crispin: The Cross of Lead	Avi	Yes
Sadako and the Thousand Paper Cranes	Coerr, Eleanor	
The Watsons Go to Birmingham—1963	Curtis, Christopher Paul	
Bud, Not Buddy	Curtis, Christopher Paul	
Catherine, Called Birdy	Cushman, Karen	
Stone Fox	Gardiner, John Reynolds	
Number the Stars	Lowry, Lois	

Title	Author	Sequel or Series?
A Boy at War	Mazer, Harry	Yes
Kensuke's Kingdom	Morpurgo, Michael	
Private Peaceful	Morpurgo, Michael	
Soldier's Heart	Paulsen, Gary	
Where the Red Fern Grows	Rawls, Wilson	
Riding Freedom	Ryan, Pam Munoz	
Esperanza Rising	Ryan, Pam Munoz	
Under the Blood-Red Sun	Salisbury, Graham	
The Wednesday Wars	Schmidt, Gary	
Homeless Bird	Whelan, Gloria	
The Ravenmaster's Secret	Woodruff, Elvira	
Hiroshima	Yep, Laurence	
The Devil's Arithmetic	Yolen, Jane	
Science Fiction		
Things Not Seen	Clements, Andrew	
The Supernaturalist	Colfer, Eoin	
The Last Dog on Earth	Ehrenhaft, Daniel	
The House of the Scorpion	Farmer, Nancy	
The Ear, the Eye, and the Arm	Farmer, Nancy	
Among the Hidden	Haddix, Margaret Peterson	Yes
Double Identity	Haddix, Margaret Peterson	
Stormbreaker	Horowitz, Anthony	Yes

Title	Author	Sequel or Series?
The Giver	Lowry, Lois	Yes
The Beasties	Sleator, William	
Cryptid Hunter	Smith, Roland	
Uglies	Westerfeld, Scott	Yes
Mystery		
Chasing Vermeer	Balliet, Blue	Yes
Half-Moon Investigations	Colfer, Eoin	
The Face on the Milk Carton	Cooney, Caroline	Yes
Last Shot: A Final Four Mystery	Feinstein, John	
From the Mixed-Up Files of Mrs. Basil E. Frankweiler	Konigsburg, E. L.	
On the Run: Chasing the Falconers	Korman, Gordon	Yes
How to Disappear Completely and Never Be Found	Nickerson, Sara	
Sammy Keyes and the Hotel Thief	Van Draanen, Wendelin	Yes
Traditional Literature		
D'Aulaire's Book of Greek Myths	D'Aulaire, Ingri	
D'Aulaire's Book of Norse Myths	D'Aulaire, Ingri	
Myths and Legends	Horowitz, Anthony	
The Rough-Face Girl	Martin, Rafe	
The Outlaws of Sherwood	McKinley, Robin	
Beast	Napoli, Donna Jo	

Title	Author	Sequel or Series?
Bound	Napoli, Donna Jo	
Favorite Greek Myths	Osborne, Mary Pope	
The Once and Future King	White, T. H.	
Greyling	Yolen, Jane	
Here There Be Dragons	Yolen, Jane	Yes
Poetry		
Love That Dog	Creech, Sharon	
If You're Not Here, Please Raise Your Hand	Dakos, Kalli	
Joyful Noise	Fleischman, Paul	
Toasting Marshmallows	George, Kristine O'Connell	
I Never Said I Wasn't Difficult	Holbrook, Sara	
Dirty Laundry Pile: Poems in Different Voices	Janeczko, Paul	
The Headless Horseman Rides Tonight	Prelutsky, Jack	
For Laughing Out Loud	Prelutsky, Jack	
Where the Sidewalk Ends	Silverstein, Shel	
A Light in the Attic	Silverstein, Shel	
One of Those Hideous Books Where the Mother Dies	Sones, Sonya	
What My Mother Doesn't Know	Sones, Sonya	
Biographies, Autobiographies, and Memoirs		
Anne Frank: The Diary of a Young Girl	Frank, Anne	

Title	Author	Sequel or Series?
Helen Keller: A Photographic Story of a Life	Garrett, Leslie	Yes
The Tarantula in My Purse	George, Jean Craighead	
Water Buffalo Days: Growing Up in Vietnam	Huynh, Quang Nhuong and Tseng, Jean & Mou-sien	
Small Steps: The Year I Got Polio	Kehret, Peg	
Tree Shaker: The Story of Nelson Mandela	Keller, Bill	
How Angel Peterson Got His Name	Paulsen, Gary	
My Life in Dog Years	Paulsen, Gary	
Guts	Paulsen, Gary	
Informational		
Hitler Youth	Bartoletti, Susan	
World War II	DK Eyewitness Books	Yes
The Way Things Work	Macaulay, David	
Castle	Macaulay, David	Yes
Oh Rats! The Story of Rats and People	Marrin, Albert and Mordan, C. B.	
You Wouldn't Want to Be an Egyptian Mummy!	Stewart, David, Salariya, David, and Antram, David	Yes

Appendix C: Student Forms

READING INTEREST-A-LYZER©

Based on the Interest-A-Lyzer by Joseph S. Renzulli

Name _____ Grade _____ Age _____

1.) Are you currently reading a book for pleasure? ❏ YES   ❏ NO

2.) Do you ever read a book for pleasure? ❏ YES   ❏ NO

3.) When I read for pleasure, I pick the following (Check all that apply):

❏ Novels/chapter books   ❏ History books   ❏ Picture books
❏ Newspapers   ❏ Sports books   ❏ Mystery books
❏ Poetry books   ❏ Fantasy books   ❏ Fiction books
❏ Cartoons/comic books   ❏ Science books   ❏ Biographies
❏ Humorous books   ❏ Scary books   ❏ Non-fiction books
❏ Magazines   ❏ Poetry books   Other

_____

4.) I am more likely to read a book for pleasure that:

❏ a teacher suggests   ❏ my friend suggests
❏ a librarian suggests   ❏ has won an award
❏ is by an author whose books   ❏ I just happened to see (hear about)
   I have read   in_____

5.) Three favorite books that I would take on a month-long trip are:

   1. _____
   2. _____
   3. _____

6.) In the past week, I have read for at least half an hour (30 minutes):

❏ No days   ❏ 1-2 days   ❏ 3-4 days   ❏ 6-7 days

7.) In the past month, I have read _____ book(s) for pleasure:

❏ No books ❏ 1 book   ❏ 2 books   ❏ 3 books   ❏ More than 3 books

8.) My favorite time to read for pleasure is:

☐ Never   ☐ In the morning before school
☐ During school   ☐ During the midmorning
☐ Lunchtime   ☐ After school
☐ In the evening   ☐ Before falling asleep
☐ Whenever I can   ☐ _____

9.) When I read I like to: ☐ read one book   ☐ read more than one book at a time

10.) I like to receive books as presents.   ☐ YES   ☐ NO

11.) I have a <u>public</u> library card.   ☐ YES   ☐ NO

12.) I borrow books from the <u>public</u> library:

☐ Once a week   ☐ Twice a week   ☐ A couple of times a month
☐ Every few months   ☐ A few times a year   ☐ Hardly ever
☐ Never

13.) I borrow books from the <u>school</u> library:

☐ Once a week   ☐ Twice a week   ☐ A couple of times a month
☐ Every few months   ☐ A few times a year   ☐ Hardly ever
☐ Never

14.) The number of books I have at home:

☐ None   ☐ 0–9   ☐ 10–19
☐ 20–29   ☐ 30–50   ☐ More than 50

15.) If I could meet any literary character (for example, Hermione from *Harry Potter* or the dog from *Because of Winn-Dixie*), I want to meet:

- _____
- _____

16.) The last three books that I have read are:

1. _____
2. _____
3. _____

17.) I would like to read a book about:

_____

Source: Reis et al., 2005. "Reading Interest-A-Lyzer." Copyright © 2005 by Sally M. Reis. Based on the *Interest-A-Lyzer* by Joseph S. Renzulli.

Characteristics of Genre

The word *genre* means type or kind. We use genres as a system to classify books by their common characteristics.

Poetry

1. _____
2. _____
3. _____
4. _____

Traditional Literature

1. _____
2. _____
3. _____
4. _____

Fantasy

1. _____
2. _____
3. _____
4. _____

Science Fiction

1. _____
2. _____
3. _____
4. _____

Realistic Fiction

1. _____
2. _____
3. _____
4. _____

Historical Fiction

1. _____
2. _____
3. _____
4. _____

Mystery

1. _____
2. _____
3. _____
4. _____

Biography, Autobiography, Memoir

1. _____
2. _____
3. _____
4. _____

Informational

1. _____
2. _____
3. _____
4. _____

End-of-Year Reading Evaluation

Directions: Please answer the following questions in as much detail as possible. I want to read your honest thoughts and opinions about reading and the design of this class.

1. What is your attitude toward reading? Has this class changed your opinion? If so, how?

    _____

    _____

    _____

    _____

    _____

    _____

    _____

2. Estimate how many books you read *independently* last school year.

    _____

    _____

    _____

3. How many books did you read independently this year? (Include all of the books that you read, even if they did not meet genre requirements.)

    _____

    _____

    _____

    _____

4. How do you feel about the amount of reading you did this year?

_____

_____

_____

_____

_____

_____

_____

5. Did you meet your genre requirements? If not, explain.

_____

_____

_____

_____

_____

6. What was the best book you read this year? Why?

_____

_____

_____

_____

_____

_____

7. Which topics, authors, series, books, etc., do you plan to read in the future?

    _____

    _____

    _____

    _____

    _____

    _____

    _____

8. What do you wish you had learned about reading this year that you did not?

    _____

    _____

    _____

    _____

    _____

    _____

9. What advice can you give readers in this class next year?

    _____

    _____

    _____

    _____

    _____

    _____

10. In the next section, put a check mark next to the elements of this class that have helped you as a reader. Circle the factor that was most important to you.

Classroom library

School librarian/
   library

Book commercials

Independent reading
   time in class

Nightly reading time at
   home

Conferences

Other: _____

Teacher who reads

Conversations with
   classmates

Book club

Reading response
   letters

Read-alouds

Book reviews

11. If you were designing the layout of the classroom library and the checkout system, what would you do to make it easier for students to use?

_____

_____

_____

_____

_____

_____

_____

_____

12. If you could tell other adults such as librarians, teachers, or parents one thing about reading and kids that they do not know, what would it be?

_____

_____

_____

_____

_____

_____

_____

_____

_____

_____

13. What obstacles do you see that might prevent you from reading in the future?

_____

_____

_____

_____

_____

_____

_____

_____

_____

_____

14. If you could design your own genre requirements, what would that look like? You must put at least two books in each category.

_____ Poetry

_____ Traditional literature

_____ Realistic fiction

_____ Biography, autobiography, memoir

_____ Historical fiction

_____ Informational

_____ Science fiction

_____ Fantasy

_____ Mystery

_____ Reader's Choice:

_____ _____

15. What other changes or additions would you make to this class to help readers in the future?

_____

_____

_____

_____

_____

_____

_____

_____

_____

_____

References

Allen, J. (2000). *Yellow brick roads: Shared and guided paths to independent reading 4–12*. Portland, ME: Stenhouse.

Allington, R. L. (1977). If they don't read much, how they ever gonna get good? *Journal of Reading* (later renamed *Journal of Adolescent and Adult Literacy*), *21*, 57–61.

Allington, R. L. (2006). *What really matters for struggling readers: Designing research-based programs*. Boston: Pearson.

Alsup, J., & Bush, J. (2003). *But will it work with real students? Scenarios for teaching secondary English language arts*. Urbana, IL: National Council of Teachers of Language Arts.

Anderson, R. C., Hiebert, C. H., Scott, J. A., & Wilkinson, I.A.G. (1985). *Becoming a nation of readers: The report of the Commission on Reading*. Washington, DC: National Institute of Education.

Applegate, A. J., & Applegate, M. D. (2004). The Peter effect: Reading habits and attitudes of preservice teachers. *Reading Teacher, 57*(6), 554–563.

Atwell, N. (1998). *In the middle: New understandings about writing, reading, and learning*. Portsmouth, NH: Heinemann.

Blasingame, J. (2007). *Books that don't bore 'em: Young adult books that speak to this generation*. New York: Scholastic.

Calkins, L. (1994). *The art of teaching writing*. Portsmouth, NH: Heinemann.

Cambourne, B. (1995). Toward an educationally relevant theory of literacy learning: Twenty years of inquiry. *Reading Teacher*, *49*(3), 182–190.

Crowe, C. (1999, September). Young adult literature. *English Journal*, *89*(1), 139.

Elmore, R. F. (2002, May). Hard questions about practice. *Educational Leadership*, *59*(8), 22–25.

Fisher, D., & Ivey, G. (2007, March). Farewell to *A Farewell to Arms*: Deemphasizing the whole-class novel. *Phi Delta Kappan*, pp. 494–497.

Fountas, I., & Pinnell, G. (2001). *Guiding readers and writers (Grades 3–6): Teaching comprehension, genre, and content literacy*. Portsmouth, NH: Heinemann.

Fram, A. (2007, August 21). One in four read no books last year. Retrieved August 22, 2007, from *The Washington Post* at http://www.washingtonpost.com/wp-dyn/content/article/2007/08/21/AR2007082101045.html

Gambrell, L. (1996). Creating classroom cultures that foster reading motivation. *Reading Teacher*, *50*(1), 14–25.

Halsted, J. W. (2002). *Some of my best friends are books: Guiding gifted readers from preschool to high school*. Scottsdale, AZ: Great Potential Press.

Jacobs, B., & Hjalmarsson, H. (Eds.). (2002). *The quotable book lover*. Guilford, CT: Lyons Press.

Keene, E., & Zimmerman, S. (1997). *Mosaic of thought: Teaching comprehension in a reader's workshop*. Portsmouth, NH: Heinemann.

Krashen, S. (2004). *The power of reading: Insights from the research*. Portsmouth, NH: Heinemann.

National Institute of Child Health and Human Development. (2000). *Report of the National Reading Panel. Teaching children to read: An evidence-based assessment of the scientific research literature on reading and its implications for reading instruction* (NIH Publication No. 00-4769). Washington, DC: U.S. Government Printing Office.

Pennac, D. (2006). *The rights of the reader*. London: Walker Books.

Quindlen, A. (1998). *How reading changed my life*. New York: Ballantine.

Reis, S. M., et al. (2005). *The Schoolwide Enrichment Model—Reading framework* (SEM-R). Storrs: National Research Center on the Gifted and Talented, University of Connecticut.

Robinson, J. (2005, December 18). Why you should read children's books as an adult. Retrieved March 30, 2008, from Jen Robinson's Book Page at http://jkrbooks.typepad.com/blog/2005/12/why_you_should_.html

Rosenblatt, L. (1969). Towards a transactional theory of reading. *Journal of Reading Behavior*, *1*(1), 31–51.

Ruddell, R. (1995). Those influential literacy teachers: Meaning negotiators and motivation builders. *Reading Teacher*, *48*(6), 454–463.

Samuels, C. A. (2007, September, 10). Experts eye solutions to "fourth grade slump." *Education Week*, *27*(3). Retrieved October 1, 2008, from http://www.edweek.org/ew/articles/2007/09/12/03slump.h27.html

Stanovich, K. E. (1986). Matthew effects in reading: Some consequences of individual differences in the acquisition of literacy. *Reading Research Quarterly*, *21*(4), 360–407.

Thomas, L., & Tchudi, S. (1999). *The English language: An owner's manual*. Boston: Allyn & Bacon.

Weaver, C. (1996). *Teaching grammar in context*. Portsmouth, NH: Boynton/Cook.

Index

Morrison, Toni, 5
Mosaic of Thought (Keene and Zimmerman), 15
Motivation: blog responses on nurturing,
175–177; book commercials for, 137–138;
book groups for, 128–129, 130; celebrating
milestones and, 78, 83, 144–146; expanding
in-class reading time and, 144; incentive
programs for, 149–150; practices deadening,
121–127; reading as own, 151; reading logs
for, 143; realigning teaching practice to, 122;
scholarship on creating, 167–168; students
feedback on, 153, 156; traditional book
reports and, 135. *See also* Encouragement
Multiple readings of books, 72
My Life in Dog Years (Paulsen), 87
Myers, Ron, 14, 64, 179–181

N

National Institute of Child Health and Human
Development, 2, 3
National Institutes of Health, 121
National Reading Panel, 2, 3
No Child Left Behind, 27

O

Oral reading: preparing and practicing, 148;
round-robin and popcorn reading,
146–147; substitutes for, 148–149. *See also*
Read-alouds
Outsiders, The (?), 125

P

Parents. *See* Adults
Paulsen, Gary, 83, 87
Peer pressure and reading, 81–82
Pennac, D., 75, 193
"Peter Effect, The" (Applegate and Applegate),
107
Philbrick, Nathaniel, 73
Philbrick, Rodman, 105–106
Picture day, 57–58
Pinnell, Gay Su, 15, 78, 95–96
Podcasts of books, 149

Poetry, 129–130
Popcorn reading, 146–147
Power of Reading, The (Krashen), 3, 51
Publishers Weekly, 138

Q

Quiet time, 67–68
Quindlen, Anna, 49

R

Rag and Bone Shop, The (Cormier), 86
Ragtime (Doctorow), 49
Read-alouds: favorite, 87; introducing, 86–88;
round-robin and popcorn reading,
146–147; whole-class novels as, 126
Readers: achievement gap for, 25; dormant,
27–30; effect of oral reading on, 146–147;
empowering book choices by, 21–23, 26–27,
31–32, 74, 82–83, 177; impact of
whole-novel teaching on, 124–125;
increasing reading time for, 24–25, 35, 51;
self-identity of, 26–27; statistics on adult,
106–107; types of, 23–24; underground,
30–32; using surveys to encourage, 39–46;
working with developing, 24–27
Reader's notebooks: creating own, 117; keeping,
95–97; using information from, 99–102
Reading: achievement gap in, 25; activities
inspiring more, 13–14; authentic, 4; books
multiple times, 72; carrying books
everywhere, 57–58, 63; children's books,
113–114; creating classroom for learning,
34–37; demotivation of, 121–122; during
classroom interruptions, 53–54; fitting
independent reading to curriculum, 17;
importance of, 52, 179–181; importance to
teacher, 108–110; incentive programs for,
149–150; increasing time for, 24–25, 35,
51; inspiring others to read, 106–108;
instilling love of, 77, 106, 123–124;
institutional support for independent,
166–168; as its own reward, 151; making
classroom place for, 63–67; opportunities

Acknowledgments

Writing a book is hard work, and not only for the writer. My greatest hope is that this book is worthy of those individuals who provided unflagging support to me during the process. We share one vision—our commitment to children and the goal of inspiring and motivating them to read.

First, I must thank my publisher, Jossey-Bass. I accepted their offer to publish this book because their earnest belief in helping teachers and students shone like a beacon from every person I met. Leslie Iura, Paul Foster, Dimi Berkner, and Christie Hakim championed the book from the beginning and gave me a great deal of leeway while writing it. I appreciate their confidence. Discovering Paul's love for *Where the Red Fern Grows* was an added bonus! Thanks also to Julia Parmer, Pamela Berkman, Carolyn Uno, Carrie Wright, and the rest of the editorial and marketing teams who worked in the trenches to bring this book to publication.

The dedicated team at teachermagazine.org gave me my start in 2007 when they hired me to write an "Ask the Mentor" column and later offered me "The Book Whisperer" blog. The seeds for this book were planted at teachermagazine.org. I am grateful to Virginia Edwards, Mary-Ellen Phelps Deily, and Anthony Rebora for their support. I also appreciate the many readers of the blog whose comments make me think and who inspire me with their teaching knowledge and consideration for the students in their classrooms. Thanks also to Jen Robinson, who regularly links to my blog on her own outstanding Web site.

To call Elizabeth Rich an editor misrepresents her contribution. Elizabeth brought me to teachermagazine.org, advocated for my work, and eased my fears about writing this book when she agreed to edit it. Every line has been filtered through her shrewd judgment and instinct for storytelling, and this book is better for it. Never afraid to push me when she thought I could do more, Elizabeth taught me how to be a writer, to look for the turtles, and to see a bigger vision for this book than I first thought possible. Thank you, E, for being not only interested, but interesting. You are more than my editor; you are family.

This book would not have been possible without my principal, Dr. Ron Myers. Ron is the epitome of an instructional leader—dedicated to his own professional growth and that of his staff. He always says, "It is about the kids, not the adults," and never allows us to lose sight of the reason we are in education—to improve the lives of children. From reading drafts, to opening his home, to writing the afterword, Ron has been a tireless promoter of this book. Ron, even though you are a University of Oklahoma fan and tell corny jokes, I will work for you as long as you will let me.

When Susie Kelley loaned me her copy of *Mosaic of Thought* all of those years ago, she put my feet on a path to better teaching. Susie is the most generous person I know, giving freely of her books, her ideas, and her friendship. Watching her teach and talking to her about instruction is like taking a master's class every day.

I am grateful to Heather Freeman and Mellie Joiner, who snuck me in to meet Janet Allen, and introduced me as an author. Also thanks to Debbie Brooks, assistant principal extraordinaire, who calls me "friend," and means it. I appreciate the many administrators and teachers of Keller Independent School District who supported the creation of this book.

I never believed I could write a book until I participated in the National Writing Project. Thanks to the leaders of the North Star of Texas chapter at the University of North Texas: Leslie Patterson,

Carol Wickstrom, Janelle Mathis, Joan Curtis, and Terisa Pearce. Special thanks to Carol, who read my book and provided advice. A shout-out to my fellow teacher consultants, who cheerfully asked me how the book was going each time we crossed paths, and especially to Audrey Wilson, Kerri Harris, and Jennifer Roberts, who kept me from getting a big head about it. You ladies are the teachers I want to be when I grow up.

Thanks to Alexandra Leavell, who taught me the difference between *research-based* and *research-proven*, and who convinced me that I could present at the National Council of Teachers of English conference. I am also grateful to Jeff Anderson, who paid it forward by sharing his experiences as a teacher and writer, and never considered me a stalker.

My husband Don knows more about teaching reading than any spouse should. He read every draft numerous times, ironed my work clothes for eight months, brought me dinner at the computer almost every night, and told me that he wished he could have been in my class. The knowledge that we will totter off into old age together, happily reading our beloved books, makes me smile from ear to ear.

I am blessed with two remarkable daughters, Celeste and Sarah, who reminded me that I needed to spend time playing dominoes and watching movies with them in order to stay sane. Thanks, girls, for sacrificing so much Mom time.

A special thanks to my mother, who taught me how to read and, in doing so, gave me everything—my education, my career, and my life's passion.

I am indebted to the marvelous students I have taught over the years. Thanks to all of the parents and students who agreed to be in the book, sent me pictures, and cheered me on. Your words and accomplishments deserve to be heard.

About the Author

DONALYN MILLER is a sixth-grade language arts and social studies teacher at Trinity Meadows Intermediate School in Keller, Texas. In her quest to spread reading freedom, Donalyn teaches staff development presentations on campuses and in conference rooms across the country. Her articles and essays appear in national publications such as *Library Sparks Magazine*. In "The Book Whisperer," her blog for teachermagazine.org, Donalyn shares her ideas and strategies for teaching reading and inspiring students to read.

Donalyn lives atop a dragon's hoard of unread books she calls "the Miller Mountain" with her husband, two daughters, and granddaughter. In her spare time, Donalyn travels, visits old friends, and daydreams—all inside the pages of her treasured books.

About the Sponsor

EDUCATION WEEK PRESS is the book publishing division of Editorial Projects in Education (EPE), home of the independent newspaper *Education Week* and other highly regarded print and online products. Among those products is teachermagazine.org, a Web site devoted to news and information for K–12 teachers and the home of Donalyn Miller's blog "The Book Whisperer." In addition to her blog, Miller's popular column "Ask the Mentor" on teachermagazine.org inspired this book. EPE is a nonprofit organization based in Bethesda, Maryland; its other entities include the EPE Research Center, edweek.org, Digital Directions, the Teacher Professional Development Sourcebook, and TopSchoolJobs.org.